Greenhouse Technology and Management

Second Edition

Greenhouse Technology and Management

Second Edition

K. RADHA MANOHAR
C. IGATHINATHANE

BSP BS Publications
An Imprint of **BSP Books Pvt. Ltd.**
4-4-309/316, Giriraj Lane,
Sultan Bazar, Hyderabad - 500 095

Greenhouse Technology and Management - ***Second Edition*** **by**
K. Radha Manohar and C. Igathinathane

37th *Reprint*, 2024

Published by :

BSP BS Publications
An Imprint of **BSP Books Pvt. Ltd.**
4-4-309/316, Giriraj Lane, Sultan Bazar,
Hyderabad - 500 095
Phone : 040 - 23445688
e-mail : info@bspbooks.net
www.bspbooks.net

Printed at
Repro India Limited.

ISBN : 978-81-7800-136-4 (Hardbound)

Preface to Second Edition

While working on the second edition of this book, an attempt was made to make this text book more valuable to the students and teachers as well. The whole book received a complete change in layout and presentation. Several new illustrations were added and many old illustrations were modified to give students a better understanding of the subject. Also based on the feedback by the students and teachers, more worked out examples were added. Answer keys to the exercise numerical problems were incorporated for the benefit of students. Additional information on Greenhouse Heating (12th Chapter) with numerical examples is also included to provide insight to the engineering graduate students on different possibilities of heat requirement calculations of greenhouses. The authors like to record their appreciation for the support and best wishes of the student community and colleagues and always welcome the feedback from the readers. The authors gratefully acknowledge the moral support of their parents and family members.

- Authors

Preface to First Edition

Greenhouse technology is an emerging field and is likely to hold the key to crop production of the future. Books of Indian origin on greenhouses in particular and protected agriculture in general are scarce. As the greenhouse and other protected agricultural technologies are at the preliminary stage, the authors believe that this book provides an overall view of the subject. This book is intended to cater to the needs of the under graduate students of agriculture, agricultural engineering, horticulture, forestry and related fields. Subject content in this book, though basically received a treatment from engineering point of view, is meant for general use. The crop cultural and related aspects also got their due consideration.

Protected agriculture and greenhouse technology is a conglomeration of various fields of agriculture, basic science and engineering. The subject draws information from the fields like agricultural sciences, agricultural engineering, horticultural sciences, civil engineering, environmental engineering, plasticulture, material science, instrumentation, computers, economics, marketing and management. This book provides briefly the introductory and basic information on all the aspects of protected agriculture. The readers are advised to refer to the primary sources and the specialised books in the field for additional information. Special emphasis is given in the book to incorporate several illustrations, wherever necessary, to provide a better insight of the subject. Brevity and language simplicity is maintained throughout the text. The authors would be grateful to receive suggestions from the readers that would be helpful for the future revisions.

The authors express their gratitude to Dr. P. Raghavulu, Dean (Agriculture), Acharya N.G. Ranga Agricultural University, Hyderabad, Dr. D. Appa Rao, Associate Dean, College of Agricultural Engineering, (ANGRAU), Bapatla for their moral support and motivation. The authors wish to record their gratitude to Dr. Pitam Chandra, Principal Scientist and Project Co-ordinator, (PDC), Division of Agricultural Engineering, IARI, New Delhi and Dr. P. K. Chattopadhyay, Chairman, Post Harvest Technology Centre, IIT, Kharagpur for their inspiration and valuable suggestions.

The author express their gratitude to Dr. Sivala Kumar, Head, Department of Agricultural Process and Food Engineering, College of Agricultural Engineering, Bapatla for the constant encouragement and suggestions. Thanks are also due to the staff of the College of Agricultural Engineering, Bapatla viz., Dr. N.R.K. Murthy, Professor and Head, Department of Farm Machinery and Power, Mr. K. Venkatramaiah, Head, Department of Agro-Energy, Mr. D.D. Smith, Dr. D. Bhaskar Rao, Mr. V. Pattabirami Reddy, Mr. K. Yella Reddy, Mr. A. Srinivasulu for their encouragement. Help rendered by Mr. M. Damodara Rao, Mr. P. Anand Kumar and Mr. M. Sudheer, in the preparation of some of the drawings is highly appreciated.

The authors wish to record their sincere thanks to Dr. C.R. Sukumaran, Principal Scientist, PHTC, Bapatla and Dr. T.V. Satyanarayana, Principal Scientist, Indo-Dutch Project, Bapatla for their co-operation. Valuable suggestions of Dr. V. Radha Krishna Murthy, Assistant Professor, College of Agriculture, Rajendranagar, Hyderabad and Dr. K.V. Seetharamaiah, Scientist and Head, Rice Research Unit, Bapatla are highly appreciated.

The authors thankfully acknowledge the co-operation extended by M/s. Book Syndicate Publishers, Hyderabad for bringing out this book in the present form. The authors are grateful to Mr. K. Pundarikakshudu, Head, Department of Physics (Retd.), SKBR College, Amalapuram for proof reading the manuscript and providing valuable editorial suggestions. The authors express their appreciation to Mr. D. Ambarisha, Digital Studio, Hyderabad for the cover design.

The best wishes and constant encouragement of Mr. G. Aravinda Reddy, Mr. C. Ramana, Dr. K. Srinivas Reddy, Dr. V. Palanimuthu, Mr. G. Sunil Kumar Babu, Mr. S. Murugane Babu, Ms. Jissy K. Jacob and Ms. Sahiram Gnanambiga Lalida is highly appreciated.

The moral support and forbearance of the family members of the authors Mrs. K.S.K. Sudha Phani, Baby Navya Sruthi, Ms. C. Saya Devy and Ms. C. Abeda Devy is highly appreciated.

- Authors

Preface to Second Edition .... (v)
Preface to First Edition .... (vii)
List of Abbreviations .... (xv)

Chapter 1
Introduction **1**
1.1 History 1
1.2 Greenhouse Effect 1
1.3 Advantages of Greenhouses 4
Review Questions 5

Chapter 2
Classification of Greenhouses **7**
2.1 Greenhouse Type Based on Shape 7
2.2 Greenhouse Type Based on Utility 11
2.3 Greenhouse Type Based on Construction 12
2.4 Greenhouse Type Based on Covering Materials 14
Review Questions 16

Chapter 3
Plant Response to Greenhouse Environment **17**
3.1 Light 17
3.2 Temperature 20
3.3 Relative Humidity 20
3.4 Ventilation 21
3.5 Carbon dioxide 21
Review Questions 22

Chapter 4
Environmental Control Inside Greenhouse **23**
4.1 Manual Controlling 24
4.2 Thermostats 24
4.3 Active Summer Cooling Systems 25
4.4 Active Winter Cooling Systems 27
4.5 Carbon dioxide Enrichment Methiods 30
Review Questions 31

Chapter 5
Greenhouse Ventilation and Computerised Control Systems **33**
5.1 Natural Ventilation 34
5.2 Forced Ventilation 37
5.3 Microprocessors 38
5.4 Computers 39
Review Questions 42

Chapter 6
Planning of Greenhouse Facility **43**
6.1 Site Selection and Orientation 44
6.2 Structural Design 44
6.3 Conversion Materials 44
Review Questions 47

Chapter 7
Greenhouse Construction Materials **49**
7.1 Wood 49
7.2 Galvanised Iron, Aluminium, Steel and Reinforced Cement Concrete 51
7.3 Glass 52
Review Questions 53

Chapter 8

Greehouse Covering Materials 55

8.1 Polyethylene Film 56
8.2 Polyvinyl Chloride Film 57
8.3 Polyester Film 58
8.4 Tefzel T^2 Film 58
8.5 Polyvinyl Chloride Rigid Panel 59
8.6 Fiberglass-Reinforced Plastic Rigid-Panel 59
8.7 Acrylic and Polycarbonate Rigid-Panel 60
Review Questions 61

Chapter 9

Construction of Typical Greenhouses 63

9.1 Design Criteria of Construction 64
9.2 Construction of Glass Greenhouses 65
9.3 Construction of Pipe Framed Greenhouses 67
Review Questions 72

Chapter 10

Construction of Low Cost Wooden Framed Plastic Film Greenhouses 75

10.1 Material Requirement 75
10.2 Preparation of Materials 76
10.3 Constructio Procedure 78
Review Questions 84

Chapter 11

Greenhouse Cooling 85

11.1 Design of Active Summer Cooling System 86
11.2 Design of Active Winter Cooling System 94
Review Questions 97

Chapter 12
Greenhouse Heating **99**
12.1 Modes of Heat Loss 100
12.2 Heating Systems 101
12.3 Heat Distribution Systems 102
12.4 Solar Heating System 103
12.5 Water and Rock Storage 104
12.6 Heat Conservation Practices 106
12.7 Heat Requirement Calculation 107
Review Questions 122

Chapter 13
Environmental Requirement of Crops and Pest Control **125**
13.1 Temperature Requirements of Horticultural Crops 126
13.2 Light Requirements of Crops and Lighting Control Methods 127
13.3 Floricultural Crops 130
13.4 Pest and Disease Control 131
13.5 Integrated Pest Management 132
Review Questions 133

Chapter 14
Greenhouse Irrigation Systems **135**
14.1 Rules of Watering 135
14.2 Hand Watering 136
14.3 Perimeter Watering 137
14.4 Overhead Sprinklers 138
14.5 Boom Watering 139
14.6 Drip Irrigation 140
Review Questions 142

Chapter 15
Greenhouse Utilisation in Off-Season **143**
15.1 Drying of Agricultural Produce 144
15.2 Curing of Tobacco 144
15.3 Future and Research Needs in Greenhouse Technology . 146
Review Questions 147

Chapter 16

Simplified Protected Agriculture Techniques - Plastic Mulches **149**

16.1 Functions and Requrements of Mulches 150
16.2 Types of Mulches 152
16.3 Plastic Mulches 154
16.4 Technique of Mulch Laying 157
16.5 Disposal of Mulches 157
Review Questions 159

Chapter 17

Simplified Protected Agriculture Techniques-Row Covers **161**

17.1 California System 162
17.2 Fernhurst System 164
17.3 Perforated Plastic Tunnels 165
17.4 Slitted Row Covers 166
17.5 Air Supported Row Covers 167
17.6 Plastic Covered Trench System 169
17.7 Floating Row Covers 170
17.8 Requirements of Row Cover Polymers 173
Review Questions 173

Chapter 18

Advanced Protected Agriculture Systems-Liquid Hydroponics **175**

18.1 Hydroponic System 175
18.2 Nutrient Film Technique 178
18.3 NFT System Cultural Procedures 183
18.4 Deep Flow Hydroponics 186
18.5 Dynamic Root Floating Hydroponic System 187
18.6 Aeroponics 189
Review Questions 190

Chapter 19
Advanced Protected Agriculture Systems - Aggregate Hydroponics **193**

19.1 Open Systems 194
19.2 Closed Systems 200
19.3 Whole-firm Recirculation 202
Review Questions 202

Chapter 20
Economics of Greenhouse Production **205**

20.1 Capital Requirements 206
20.2 Economics of Production 207
20.3 Conditions Influencing Returns 207
Review Questions 209

Bibliography **211**

Index **213**

List of Abbreviations

BTU	-	British Thermal Unit
CAST	-	Council for Agricultural Science and Technology
CEA	-	Controlled Environment Agriculture
cmm	-	Cubic meters per minute
DIF	-	Temperature differential
DRF	-	Dynamic Root Floating
EC	-	Electrical Conductivity
FRP	-	Fiberglass Reinforced Plastic
GI	-	Glavanized Iron
HAF	-	Horizontal Air Flow
HDPE	-	High Density Polyethylene
HID	-	High Intensity Discharge
IPM	-	Integrated Pest Management
IR	-	Infrared
IRT	-	Infra Red Transmitting
LDPE	-	Low Density Polyethylene
LLDPE	-	Extra Low Density Polyethylene
lpm	-	Liters per minute
mil	-	Thousandth of an inch
MS	-	Mild Steel
NFT	-	Nutrient Film Technique
NGMA	-	National Greenhouse Manufacturers Association
OFA	-	Open Field Agriculture
PAR	-	Photosynthetically Active Radiation
ppm	-	Parts per million
RH	-	Relative Humidity
UV	-	Ultraviolet

Chapter 1

INTRODUCTION

After the advent of green revolution, more emphasis is laid on the quality of the product along with the quantity of production to meet the ever-growing food requirements. Both these demands can be met when the environment for the plant growth is suitably controlled. The need to protect the crops against unfavourable environmental conditions led to the development of protected agriculture. Greenhouse is the most practical method of achieving the objectives of protected agriculture, where the natural environment is modified by using sound engineering principles to achieve optimum plant growth and yields. In this chapter, the history, the phenomenon of greenhouse effect and advantages of greenhouses are discussed.

1.1 History

A greenhouse is a framed or an inflated structure covered with a transparent or translucent material in which crops could be grown under the conditions of at least partially controlled environment and which is large enough to permit persons to work within it to carry out cultural operations.

The growing of off-season cucumbers under transparent stone for Emperor Tiberius, in the first century, is the earliest reported protected agriculture. The technology was rarely employed during the next 1500 years. In the 16th century, glass lanterns, bell jars and hot beds covered with glass were used to protect horticultural crops against cold. In the 17th century, low portable wooden frames covered with an oiled translucent paper were used to warm the plant environment.

In Japan, straw mats were used in combination with oil paper to protect crops from the severe environmental conditions. Greenhouses in France and England during the same century were heated by manure and covered with glass panes. The first greenhouse in the 1700s used glass on one side only as a sloping roof. Later in the century, glass was used on both sides. Glasshouses were used for fruit crops such as melons, grapes, peaches and strawberries, and rarely for vegetable production. Protected agriculture was fully established with the introduction of polyethylene after the World War II. The first use of polyethylene as a greenhouse cover was in 1948, when Professor Emery Myers Emmert, at the University of Kentucky, USA, used the less expensive material in place of more expensive glass (Fig. 1.1).

Fig. 1.1 Interior view of a typical plastic greenhouse.

The total area of glasshouses in the world as per 1987 reports was estimated to be 30,000 ha and most of these were found in North-Western Europe. In contrast to glasshouses, plastic greenhouses have been readily adopted in all five continents, especially in the Mediterranean region, China and Japan. According to 1987-88 estimates, an area of 1,91,500 ha was under plastic greenhouses (Table 1.1).

In India, the cultivation in the plastic greenhouse is of recent origin. As per 1994-95 estimates, approximately 100 ha of land are under greenhouse cultivation.

Table 1.1 Estimated World Use of Plastic Greenhouses (1987-1988).

Region	Area (ha)
Western Europe	56,500
Eastern Europe	17,000
Africa and the Middle East	16,000
Americas	9,000
Asia and Oceania	93,000
World Total	191,500

Source: Jensen and Malter (1995)

Since 1960, the greenhouse has evolved into more than a plant protector. At present even at households, individual pots of plant can be given the greenhouse protection (Fig. 1.2). It is now better understood as a system of controlled environment agriculture (CEA), with precise control of air and root temperature, water, humidity, plant nutrition, carbon dioxide and light. The greenhouses of today can be considered as plant or vegetable factories. Almost every aspect of the production system is automated, with the artificial environment and growing system under nearly total computer control.

Fig. 1.2 Single pot replaceable greenhouse hoods.

1.2 Greenhouse Effect

In general, the percentage of carbon dioxide in the atmosphere is 0.0345% (345 ppm). But due to the emission of pollutants and exhaust gases into the atmosphere, the percentage of carbon dioxide increases which forms a blanket in the outer atmosphere. This causes the entrapping of the reflected solar radiation from the earth surface. Due to this, the atmospheric temperature increases, causing global warming, melting of ice caps and rise in the ocean levels which result in the submergence of coastal lines. This phenomenon of increase in the ambient temperature, due to the formation of the blanket of carbon dioxide is known as greenhouse effect. The greenhouse covering material acts in a similar way, as it is transparent to short wave radiation and opaque to long wave radiation. During the daytime the short wave radiation enters into the greenhouse and gets reflected from the ground surface. This reflected radiation becomes long wave radiation and is entrapped inside the greenhouse by the covering material. This causes the increase in- the greenhouse temperature. It is a desirable effect from point of view of crop growth in the cold regions.

1.3 Advantages of Greenhouses

The following are the advantages of using the greenhouse for growing crops under controlled environment:

1. Throughout the year four to five crops can be grown in a greenhouse due to the availability of required plant environmental conditions.
2. The productivity of the crop is increased considerably.
3. Superior quality produce can be obtained as they are grown under suitably controlled environment.
4. Gadgets for efficient use of various inputs like water, fertilizers, seeds and plant protection chemicals can be well maintained in a greenhouse.
5. Effective control of pests and diseases is possible as the growing area is enclosed.
6. Percentage of germination of seeds is high in greenhouses.
7. The acclimatization of plantlets of tissue culture technique can be carried out in a greenhouse.
8. Agricultural and horticultural crop production schedules can be planned effectively to take advantage of the market needs.
9. Different types of growing medium like peat mass, vermiculate, rice hulls and compost that are used in intensive agriculture can be effectively utilized in the greenhouse.
10. Export quality produce meeting international standards can be produced in a greenhouse.
11. When the crops are not grown, drying and related operations of the harvested produce can be taken up utilizing the entrapped heat.
12. Greenhouses are suitable for automation of irrigation, application of other inputs, and environmental controls by using computers and artificial intelligence techniques.
13. Self-employment for educated youth on farm can be increased.

REVIEW QUESTIONS

1. What circumstances lead to the development of protected agriculture?
2. Define greenhouse.
3. Write a note on the history of protected agriculture and evolution of greenhouse.
4. What is greenhouse effect and explain how the atmospheric phenomenon is applied to greenhouse structure?
5. What are the advantages of using greenhouses?

Chapter 2

CLASSIFICATION OF GREENHOUSES

Greenhouse structures of various types are used successfully for crop production. Although there are specific advantages in each type for a particular application, in general there is no single type greenhouse, which can be considered as the best. Different types of greenhouses are designed to meet the specific needs. In this chapter, different types of greenhouses based on shape, utility, construction and covering materials are briefly described.

2.1 Greenhouse Type Based on Shape

Greenhouses can be classified based on their shape or style. For the purpose of classification, the uniqueness of the cross section of the greenhouses can be utilized. As the longitudinal section tend to be approximately the same for all types, the longitudinal section of the greenhouse cannot be used for classification. The cross sections depict the width and height of the structure and the length is perpendicular to the plane of cross section. Also the cross section provides information on the overall shape of the structural members, such as truss or hoop that will be repeated on every bay. The commonly followed types of greenhouse based on shape are lean-to, even span, uneven span, ridge and furrow, saw tooth and quonset.

2.1.1 Lean-toType Greenhouse

A lean-to design is used when the greenhouse is placed against the side of an existing building (Fig. 2.1). This design makes the best use of sunlight and minimizes the requirement of roof supports. The roof of the building is extended with appropriate greenhouse covering material and the area is properly enclosed.

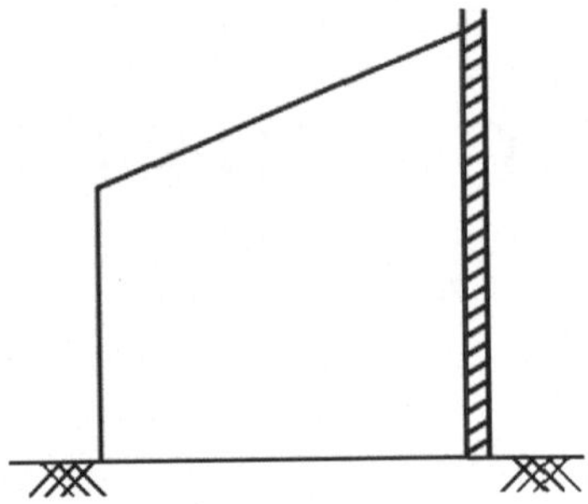

Fig. 2.1 Lean-to type greenhouse.

2.1.2 Even Span Type Greenhouse

In this type, the two roof slopes are of equal pitch and width (Fig. 2.2). This design is used for the greenhouse of small size, and it is constructed on leveled ground. Several single and multiple span types are available for use in various regions of India. For single span type, the span in general varies from 5 to 9 m, whereas the length is around 24 m. The height varies from 2.5 to 4.3 m.

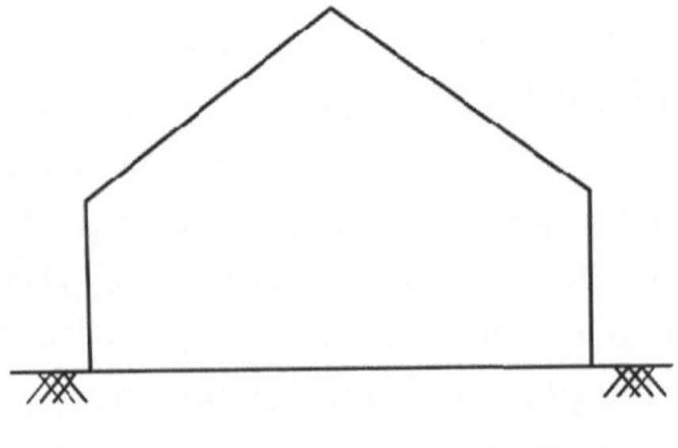

Fig. 2.2 Even span type greenhouse.

2.1.3 Uneven Span Type Greenhouse

This type of greenhouse is constructed on hilly terrain. The roofs are of unequal width, which make the structure adaptable to the side slopes of hill (Fig. 2.3). This type of greenhouses is seldom used now-a-days as it is not adaptable for automation.

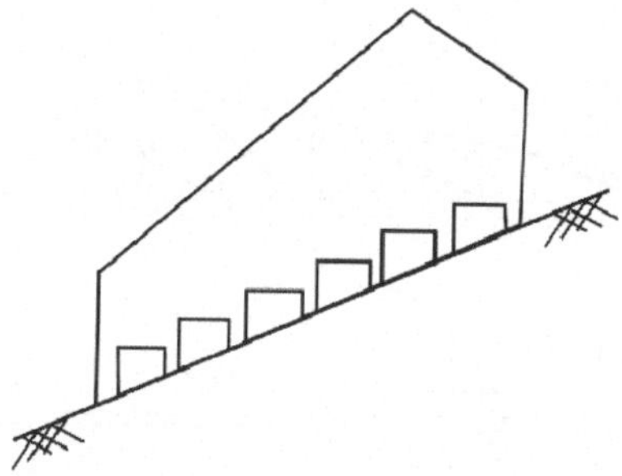

Fig. 2.3 Uneven span type greenhouse.

2.1.4 Ridge and Furrow Type Greenhouse

Designs of this type use two or more A-frame greenhouses connected to one another along the length of the eave (Fig. 2.4). The eave serves as a furrow or gutter to carry rain and melted snow away. The side walls are eliminated between the greenhouses, which results in a structure with a single large interior. Consolidation of interior space reduces labour, lowers the cost of automation, improves personal management and reduces fuel consumption, as there is less exposed wall area through which heat escapes. The snow loads must be taken into account in the frame specifications of these greenhouses since the snow cannot slide off the roofs as in case of individual free standing greenhouses, but melts away. In spite of snow loads, ridge and furrow greenhouses are effectively used in northern countries of Europe and in Canada and are well suited to the Indian conditions.

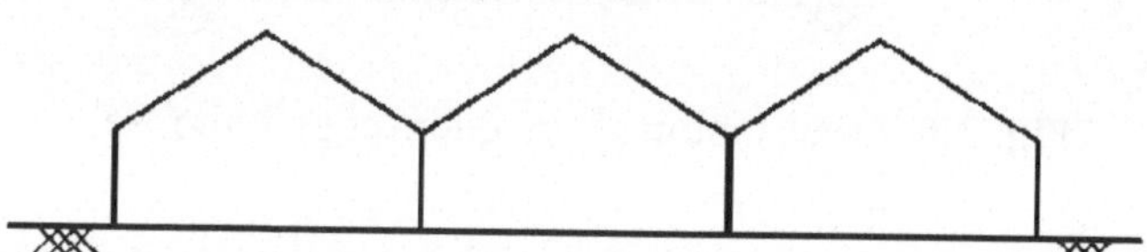

Fig. 2.4 Ridge and furrow type greenhouse.

2.1.5 Saw Tooth Type Greenhouse

These are also similar to the ridge and furrow type greenhouses except that, there is provision for natural ventilation in this type. Specific natural ventilation flow path (Fig. 2.5) develops in a saw tooth type greenhouse.

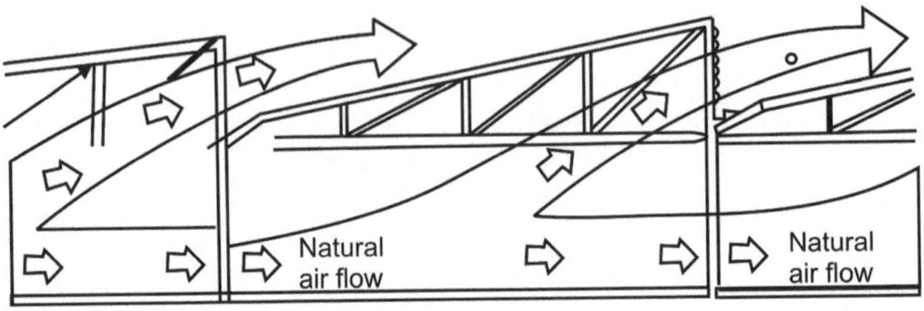

Fig. 2.5 Saw tooth type greenhouse showing air flow path in natural ventilation.

2.1.6 Quonset Greenhouse

In quonset greenhouse, the pipe arches or trusses are supported by pipe purlins running along the length of the greenhouse (Fig. 2.6). In general, the covering material used for this type of greenhouses is polyethylene. Such greenhouses are typically less expensive than the gutter connected greenhouses and are useful when a small isolated cultural area is required. These houses are connected either in free standing style or arranged in an interlocking ridge and furrow (Fig. 2.7).

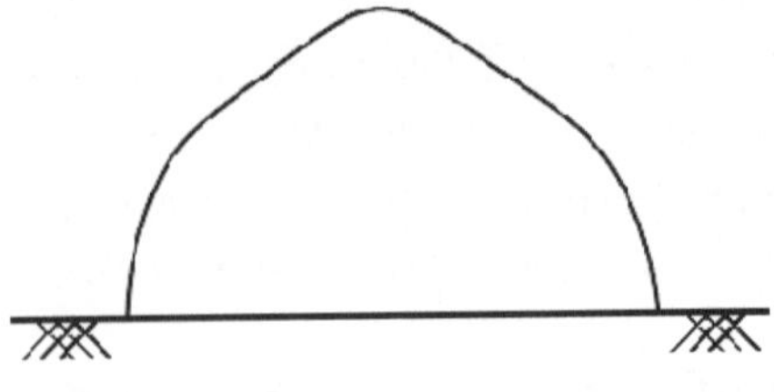

Fig. 2.6 Free standing type quonset greenhouse.

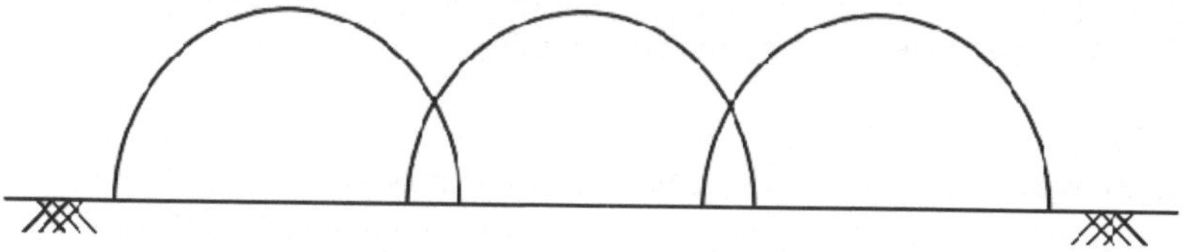

Fig. 2.7 Interlocking ridge and furrow type Quonset greenhouse.

In the interlocking type greenhouses, truss members overlap sufficiently to allow a bed of plants to grow between the overlapping portions of adjacent houses. A single large cultural space thus exists for a set of houses in this type, an arrangement that is better adapted to the automation and movement of labourers (Fig. 2.8).

Fig. 2.8 Interior view of interlocking ridge and furrow type Quonset greenhouse.

2.2 Greenhouse Type Based on Utility

Classification of greenhouses can also be made depending on the functions or utilities. Of the different utilities, artificial cooling and heating of the greenhouse are more expensive and elaborate. Hence based on the artificial cooling and heating, greenhouses are classified as that uses active heating system and active cooling system.

2.2.1 *Greenhouses for Active Heating*

During the night time, the air temperature inside greenhouse decreases and to avoid the cold bite to plants due to freezing, some amount of heat has to be supplied. The requirements for heating greenhouse depend on the rate at which the heat is lost to the outside environment. Various methods are adopted to reduce the heat losses, namely, using double layer polyethylene, thermopane glasses (two layers of factory sealed glass with dead air space) or to use heating systems, such as unit heaters, central heat, radiant heat and solar heating system.

2.2.2 *Greenhouses for Active Cooling*

During summer season, it is desirable to reduce the temperatures of greenhouse than the ambient temperatures, for effective crop growth. Hence suitable modifications are made so that large volumes of cooled air are drawn into greenhouse. This type of greenhouse either consists of evaporative cooling pad with fan or fog cooling. This greenhouse is designed in such a way that it permits a roof opening of 40% and in some cases nearly 100%.

2.3 Greenhouse Type Based on Construction

The type of construction is predominantly influenced by the structural material, though the covering materials also influence the type. Span of the house in turn dictates the selection of structural members and their construction. Higher the span, stronger should be the material and more structural members are used to make sturdy truss type frames. For smaller spans, simpler designs like hoops can be followed. Therefore based on construction, greenhouses can be broadly classified as wooden framed, pipe framed and truss framed structures.

2.3.1 *Wooden Framed Structures*

In general, for greenhouses with span less than 6 m, only wooden framed structures are used. Side posts and columns are constructed of wood without the use of a truss. Pine wood is commonly used as it is inexpensive and possesses the required strength. Timber locally available, with good strength, durability and machinability also can be used for the construction.

2.3.2 Pipe Framed Structures

When the clear span is around 12 m, pipes are used for the construction of greenhouses (Fig. 2.9). In general, the side posts, columns, cross-ties and purlins are constructed using pipes. Trusses are not used also in this type of greenhouse. The pipe components are not interconnected but depend on the attachment to the sash bars for support.

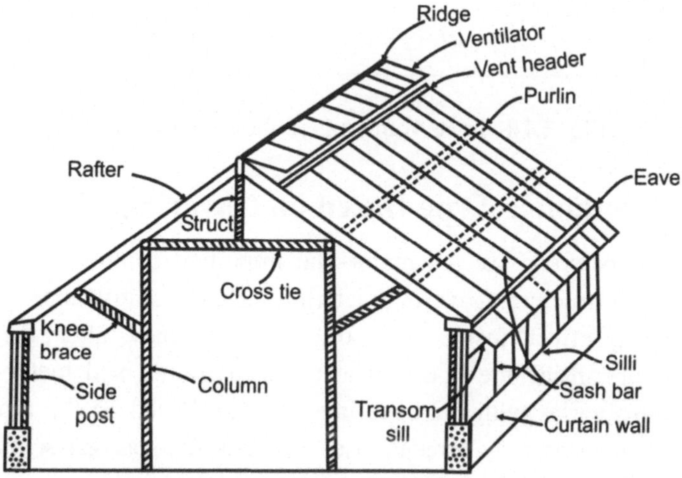

Fig. 2.9 Pipe framed greenhouse structure.

2.3.3 Truss Framed Structures

If the greenhouse span is greater than or equal to 15 m, truss frames are used (Fig. 2.10). Flat steel, tubular steel or angle iron is welded together to form a truss encompassing rafters, chords and struts. Struts are support members under compression and chords are support members under tension. Angle iron purlins running throughout the length of greenhouse are bolted to each truss. Columns are used only in very wide truss frame houses of 21.3 m or more. Most of the glass houses are of truss frame type, as these frames are best suited for pre-fabrication.

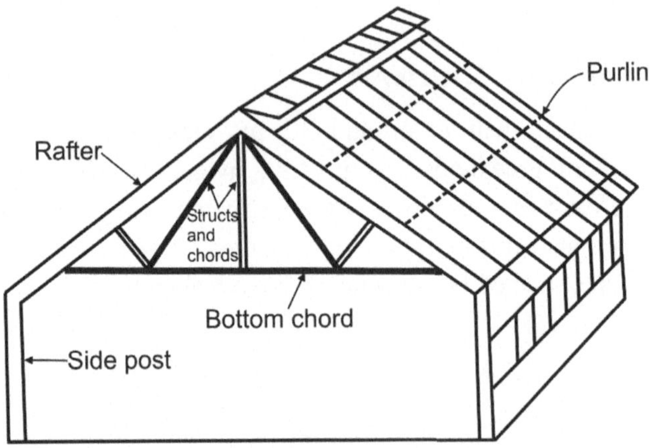

Fig. 2.10 Truss framed greenhouse structure.

2.4 Greenhouse Type Based on Covering Materials

Covering materials are the major and important component of the greenhouse structure. Covering materials have direct influence on the greenhouse effect inside the structure, and they alter the air temperature inside the house. The types of frames and method of fixing also varies with the covering material. Based on the type of covering materials the greenhouses are classified as glass, plastic film and rigid panel greenhouses.

2.4.1 Glass Greenhouses

Only glass greenhouses with glass as the covering material existed prior to 1950. Glass as covering material has the advantage of greater interior light intensity. These greenhouses have higher air infiltration rate, which leads to lower interior humidity and better disease prevention. Lean-to type, even span, ridge and furrow type of designs are used for construction of glass greenhouse.

2.4.2 Plastic Film Greenhouses

Flexible plastic films including polyethylene, polyester and polyvinyl chloride are used as covering material in this type of greenhouses. Plastics as covering material for greenhouses have become popular, as they are cheap and the cost of heating is less when compared to glass greenhouses. The main disadvantage with plastic films is its short life as the covering material. For example, the best quality ultraviolet (UV) stabilized film can last for four years only. Quonset design (Fig. 2.11) as well as gutter-connected design is suitable for using this covering material.

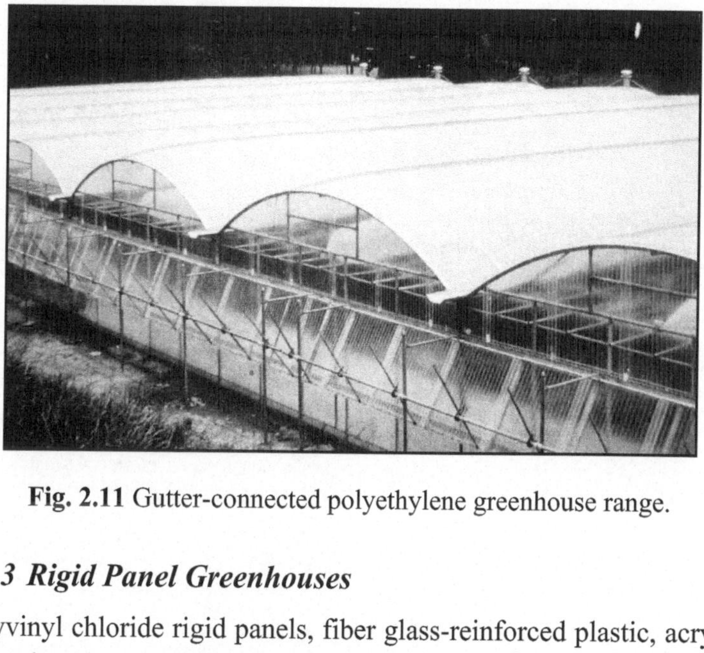

Fig. 2.11 Gutter-connected polyethylene greenhouse range.

2.4.3 Rigid Panel Greenhouses

Polyvinyl chloride rigid panels, fiber glass-reinforced plastic, acrylic and polycarbonate rigid panels are employed as the covering material in this type of greenhouses. These panels can be used in the quonset type frames or ridge and furrow type frames. This material is more resistant to breakage and the light intensity is uniform throughout the greenhouse when compared to glass or plastic. High grade panels have long life even up to 20 years. The main disadvantage is that these panels tend to collect dust as well as to harbor algae, which results in darkening of the panels and subsequent reduction in the light transmission. There is significant danger of fire hazard.

REVIEW QUESTIONS

1. Classify the greenhouses based on shape, utility, construction and covering material.
2. Give the sketches of the cross section of greenhouses based on shape.
3. What is active summer and active winter cooling of greenhouses?
4. Differentiate among wooden, pipe and truss framed structures.
5. Write short notes on glass, plastic and rigid panel as greenhouse covering material.

Chapter 3

PLANT RESPONSE TO GREENHOUSE ENVIRONMENT

The productivity of a crop is influenced not only by its heredity but also by the micro-climate around it. The components of crop micro-climate are light, temperature, air compositions and the nature of the root medium. In open fields, only manipulation of the nature of the root medium by tillage, irrigation and fertilizer applications is possible. Even in this case, the nature of the root medium is modified but not controlled. Greenhouse, however, due to its closed boundaries, permits control of any one or more of the components of the micro-climate. This chapter deals with the plant response to environment parameters, such as, light, temperature, relative humidity and ventilation.

3.1 Light

The visible light of the solar radiation is a source of energy for plants. Light energy, carbon dioxide (CO_2) and water all enter into the process of photosynthesis through which carbohydrates are formed. The production of carbohydrates from carbon dioxide and water in the presence of chlorophyll, using light energy is responsible for plant growth and reproduction. The rate of photosynthesis is governed by available fertilizer elements, water, carbon dioxide, light and temperature (Fig. 3.1).

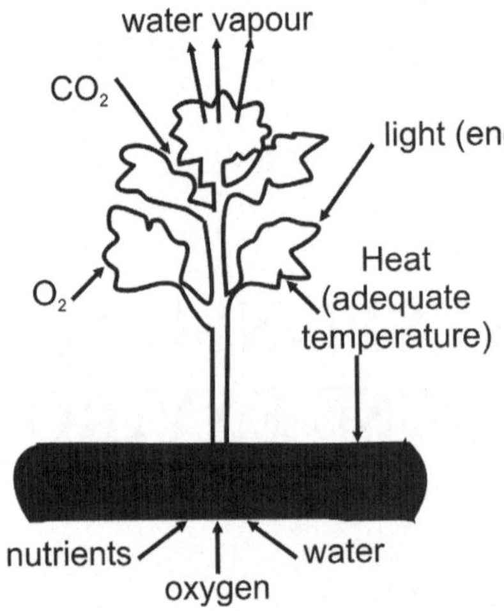

Fig. 3.1 Micro-climatic components influencing the plant growth.

The photosynthesis reaction can be represented as follows:

$$CO_2 + \text{Water} + \text{Light energy} \xrightarrow[\text{Plant nutrients}]{\text{Chlorophyll}} \text{Carbohydrate} + \text{Oxygen}$$

Considerable energy is required to reduce the carbon that is combined with oxygen in CO_2 gas to the state in which it exists in the carbohydrate. The light energy thus utilized is trapped in the carbohydrate. If the light intensity is diminished, photosynthesis slows down and hence the growth. If higher than optimal light intensities are provided, growth again slows down because of the injury to the chloroplasts.

The light intensity is measured by the international unit known as lux. It is the direct illumination on a surrounding surface that is 1 m from a uniform point source of 1 international candle. Greenhouse crops are subjected to light intensities varying from 129.6 klux on clear summer days to 3.2 klux on cloudy winter days. For most crops, neither condition is ideal. Many crops become light-saturated, in other words, photosynthesis does not increase at light intensities higher than

32.3 klux. Rose and carnation plants will grow well under full summer light intensities. For most other crops, foliage is deeper green if the greenhouse is shaded to the extent of about 40% from midspring (May) to midfall (Aug. and Sep.). Thus, it is apparent that light intensity requirements of photosynthesis vary considerably from crop to crop.

Light is classified according to its wavelength in nanometers (nm). Not all light is useful in the photosynthesis process. UV light is available in the short wavelength range, i.e. less than 400 nm. Large quantities of it are also harmful to the plants. Glass screens are opaque to most UV light and light below the range of 325 nm. Visible and white light has wavelengths of 400 to 700 nm (Fig. 3.2).

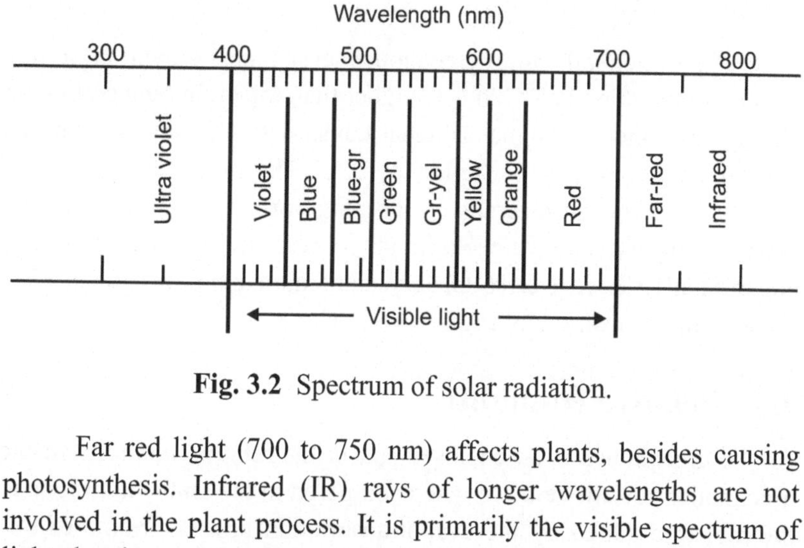

Fig. 3.2 Spectrum of solar radiation.

Far red light (700 to 750 nm) affects plants, besides causing photosynthesis. Infrared (IR) rays of longer wavelengths are not involved in the plant process. It is primarily the visible spectrum of light that is used in photosynthesis. In the blue and red bands the photosynthetic activity is higher. When the blue light (shorter wavelengths) alone is supplied to plants, the growth is retarded, and the plant becomes hard and dark in colour. When plants are grown under red light (longer wavelengths), growth is soft and internodes are long, resulting in tall plants. Visible light of all wavelengths is readily utilized in photosynthesis.

3.2 Temperature

Temperature is a measure of the level of heat present. All crops have a temperature range in which they can grow well. Below this range, the plant life processes stop due to ice formation within the tissue tying up water, and cells are possibly punctured by ice crystals. At the upper extreme, enzymes become inactive, and again the enzyme controlled processes essential for life cease. Enzymes are biological reaction catalyst and are heat sensitive. All biochemical reactions in the plant are controlled by the enzymes. The rate of reactions controlled by the enzyme often doubles or triples for each rise of temperature by 10°C, until an optimum temperature is reached. Further increase in temperature begins to suppress the reaction and finally stops it.

As a general rule, greenhouse crops are grown at a day temperature, which is 3°C to 6°C higher than the night temperature on cloudy days and 8°C higher on clear days. With CO_2 enrichment, the day temperatures may be higher by 3°C. The night temperature of greenhouse crops is generally in the range of 7°C to 21°C. Primula, mathiola incana and calceolaria grow best at 7°C carnation and cineraria at 10°C, rose at 16°C, chrysanthemum and poinsettia at 17°C to 18°C and african violet at 21°C to 22°C.

3.3 Relative Humidity

As the greenhouse is an enclosed space, the relative humidity of the greenhouse air will be more when compared to the ambient air, due to the moisture added by the evapotranspiration process. Some of this moisture is taken away by the air leaving from the greenhouse due to ventilation. Sensible heat inputs also lower the relative humidity of the air to some extent. In order to maintain desirable relative humidity levels in greenhouses, processes like humidification or dehumidification are carried out. For most crops, the acceptable range of relative humidity is between 50 to 80%. However, for plant propagation work, relative humidity up to 90% may be desirable.

In summers due to sensible heat addition in the daytime, and in winters for increasing the nighttime temperature of the greenhouse air, more sensible heat is added that causes a reduction in the relative humidity of the air. For the purpose of maintaining relative humidiy levels, evaporative cooling pads and fogging systems of humidification are employed. When the relative humidity is on the higher side, ventilators, chemical dehumidifiers and cooling coils are used for dehumidification.

3.4 Ventilation

A greenhouse is ventilated for either reducing the temperature of greenhouse air, or for replenishing carbon dioxide supply, or for moderating the relative humidity of the air. Air temperatures above 35°C are generally not suited to crops in greenhouse. It is quite possible to bring greenhouse air temperature below this upper limit during spring and autumn seasons by simply providing adequate ventilation for the greenhouse. The ventilation in a greenhouse can either be natural or forced. In case of small greenhouses (less than 6 m wide) natural ventilation can be quite effective during spring and autumn seasons. However, forcd ventilation using fans is essential for precise control over the air temperature, humidity and carbon dioxide levels.

3.5 Carbon Dioxide

Carbon is an essential plant nutrient which is present in greater quantity than any other nutrient in the plant. About 40% of the dry matter of plants is composed of carbon, and carbon dioxide (CO_2) gas in the air is the important source of carbon to plants. Under normal conditions, CO_2 exits as a gas in the atmosphere slightly above 0.03% or 345 ppm. During the day, when photosynthesis occurs under natural light, the plants in a greenhouse draw down the level of CO_2 to below 200 ppm. Under these circumstances, infiltration or ventilation increases CO_2 levels, where the outside air is brought in to maintain the CO_2 at ambient levels. If the level of CO_2 is less than ambient levels, CO_2 will become the factor of retarding the plant growth. In cold climates, maintaining ambient levels of CO_2 by providing ventilation may be uneconomical, due to the necessity of heating the incoming air in order to maintain proper growing temperatures. In such regions, enrichment of the greenhouse with CO_2 is followed. The exact CO_2 level needed for a given crop will vary, since it must be correlated with other variables in greenhouse production such as light, temperature, nutrient levels, cultivar and degree of maturity. Most crops will respond favourably to CO_2 at 1000 to 1200 ppm.

REVIEW QUESTIONS

1. What are the micro-climatic factors that influence the crop growth and how they are controlled in protected environments like greenhouse?
2. What is the unit of light intensity and define it?
3. Explain the solar radiation energy spectrum with reference to photosynthetically active radiation.
4. How temperature changes affect the plant growth processes?
5. Write short notes on:
   (a) Relative Humidity
   (b) Greenhouse ventilation
   (c) Carbon dioxide levels in greenhouse

Chapter 4

ENVIRONMENT CONTROL INSIDE GREENHOUSE

Precise control of different parameters of greenhouse environment is necessary to optimize energy inputs and, thereby, maximize the economic returns. Basically, the objective of environmental control is to maximize the plant growth. The control of greenhouse environment means the control of temperature, light, air composition and nature of the root medium. A greenhouse is essentially meant to permit at least partial control of microclimate the greenhouse encloses. Obviously, greenhouses with partial environmental control are more common and economical than full fledged systems. From the origin of greenhouses to the present, there has been a steady evolution of environmental control systems. Five stages in this evolution include manual controls, thermostats, step controllers, dedicated microprocessors and computers. This chain of evolution has brought about a reduction in control labour and an improvement in the conformity of greenhouse environments to their set points. The benefits achieved from greenhouse environmental uniformity are better timing of crops, higher quality of crops, disease control and conservation of energy. In this chapter manual and thermostat methods of environment control, active summer cooling systems, active winter cooling systems, and different CO_2 enrichment methods are described.

4.1 Manual Controlling

During the first half of the 20th century, it was common for greenhouse firms to employ a night watch person to regulate temperature. This person made periodic trips through the greenhouses during the night, checking the temperature in each greenhouse and controlling it by opening or closing valves of heating pipes as required. During the day, employees opened or closed ventilators by hand to maintain temperature. Hence the temperatures had to be manually controlled throughout the day during the cropping season. Obviously, there were large deviations on both sides from the desired temperatures, and the success of manual control was mainly based on the skill and experience of the operator.

4.2 Thermostats

Thermostat is an automatic device which senses the temperature and activates / deactivates the attached equipment, with reference to a set temperature. The thermostat may make use of bimetallic Strip or thin metal tube filled with liquid or gas as sensor and it produced some physical displacement according to the sensed temperature. These sensors activate a mechanical switch by differential expansion of bimetallic strip or by the movement of the tube due to change in the volume of gas or liquid. Though efficient, the thermostats are not highly accurate and need frequent calibration. For more accurate measurement and control of temperatures, microprocessor and computer based systems using thermocouples or thermistors as sensor are used. A thermistor is a solid-state integrated circuit chip that changes the output voltage according to temperature change. Whereas, a thermocouple consists of two dissimilar metallic wires joined together to form a junction and produces voltage variation in combination with another reference junction, proportional to the temperature difference between the two junctions. These sensors require an electronic circuit to carry the signal to a conventional switch or relay.

4.3 Active Summer Cooling Systems

Active summer cooling is achieved by evaporative cooling process. The evaporative cooling systems are developed to reduce the problem of excess heat in greenhouse. In this process, cooling takes place when the heat required for moisture evaporation is derived from the greenhouse surrounding environment causing a depression in its temperature. The two active summer cooling systems in use presently are fan-and-pad and fog systems. In the evaporative cooling process, the cooling is possible only up to the wet bulb temperature of the incoming air.

4.3.1 Fan-and-Pad Cooling System

The fan-and-pad evaporative cooling system has been available since 1954 and is still the most common summer cooling system in greenhouses. Along one wall of the greenhouse, water is passed through a pad that is usually placed vertically in the wall (Fig. 4.1). Traditionally, the pad was composed of excelsior (wood shreds), but today it is usually made of a cross-fluted cellulose material somewhat similar in appearance to corrugated cardboard.

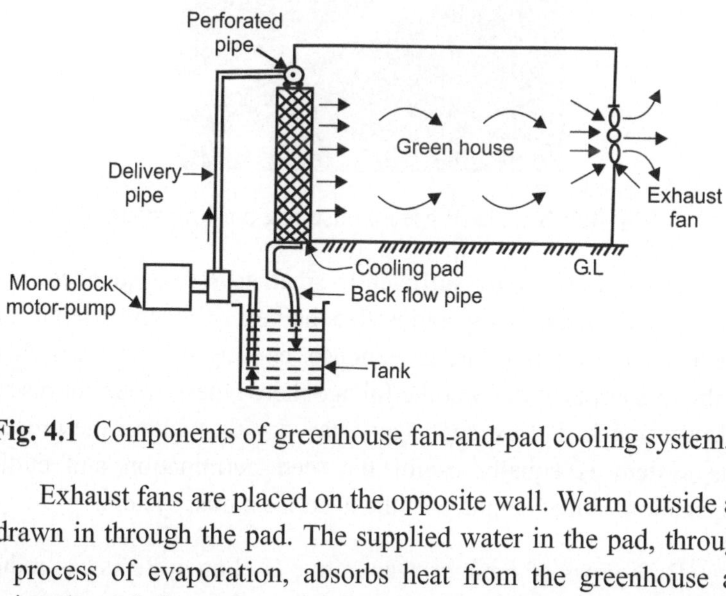

Fig. 4.1 Components of greenhouse fan-and-pad cooling system.

Exhaust fans are placed on the opposite wall. Warm outside air is drawn in through the pad. The supplied water in the pad, through the process of evaporation, absorbs heat from the greenhouse air passing through the pad as well as from the surroundings of the pad and frame, thus causing the cooling effect. Khus-khus grass mats can also be used as cooling pads.

4.3.2 Fog Cooling System

The fog evaporative cooling system, introduced in greenhouses in 1980, operates on the same cooling principle as the fan-and-pad system but uses quite a different arrangement. A high-pressure pumping apparatus generates fog containing water droplets with a mean size of less than 10 microns using suitable nozzles (Fig. 4.2).

Fig. 4.2 Nozzle of greenhouse fog cooling system.

These droplets are sufficiently small to stay suspended in air while they are evaporating and utilize the heat of greenhouse air. Fog is dispersed throughout the greenhouse, cooling the air everywhere. As this system does not wet the foliage there is less scope for disease and pest attack. People and plants stay dry throughout the process. This system is equally useful for seed germination and cutting propagation, since it eliminates the need for a mist system.

Both types of summer evaporative cooling systems can reduce the greenhouse air temperature well below the outside temperature.

The fan-and-pad system can lower the temperature of incoming air by about 80% of the difference between the dry and wet bulb temperatures, while the fog cooling system can lower the temperature by nearly the 100% of difference. This is due to the fact that complete evaporation of the water is not taking place because of bigger droplet size in fan-and-pad, whereas in the fog cooling system, there will be complete evaporation because of the minute size of the water droplets. Thus, lesser the dryness of the air, greater evaporative cooling is possible.

4.4 Active Winter Cooling Systems

Excess heat can be a problem during the winter. In the winter, the ambient temperature will be below the desired air temperature of greenhouse. Owing to the greenhouse effect, the entrapment of solar heat can raise the inside temperature to an injurious level if the greenhouse is not ventilated. Winter cooling is essentially tempering the excessively cold ambient air before it reaches the plant zone. Otherwise, hot and cold spots in the greenhouse, because of non-uniform temperature conditions, will lead to uneven crop timing and quality. The actual process of winter cooling is the mixing of low temperature ambient air with warm inside air, which cools the greenhouse environment. Two active winter cooling systems commonly employed are convection tube cooling and horizontal air flow fan cooling systems.

4.4.1 Convection Tube Cooling

The general components of convection tube are the louvered air inlet, a polyethylene convection tube with air distribution holes, a pressurizing fan to direct air into the tube under pressure and an exhaust fan to create vacuum (Fig. 4.3). When the air temperature inside the greenhouse exceeds the set point, the exhaust fan starts functioning thus creating the vacuum inside the greenhouse. The louver of the inlet in the gable is then opened, through which cold air enters due to the vacuum. The pressurizing fan, at the end of the clear polyethylene convection tube, operates to pick up the cool air entering the louver. A proper gap is available for air entry, as the end of the convection tube is separated from the louvered inlet by 0.3 to 0.6 m and the other end of the tube is sealed. Round holes of 5 to 8 cm in diameter are provided in pairs at opposite sides of the tube spaced at 0.5 to 1 m along the length of the tube.

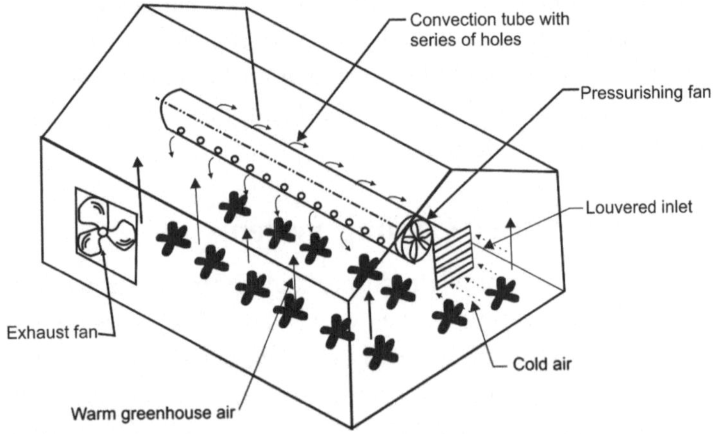

Fig. 4.3 Convection tube type active winter cooling system.

Cold air under pressure in the convection tube shoots out of holes on either side of the tube in turbulent jets. In this system, the cold air mixes with the warm greenhouse air well above the plant height. The cool mixed air, being heavier gently flows down to the floor level, effects the complete cooling of the plant area. The pressurizing fan forcing the incoming cold air into the convection tube must be capable of moving at least the same volume of air as that of the exhaust fan, thereby avoiding the development of cold spots in the house. When cooling is not required, the inlet louver closes and the pressurizing fan continues to circulate the air within the greenhouse. This process minimizes the temperature gradient at different levels. The circulation of air using convection tube consumes more power than horizontal fan circulation system.

4.4.2 Horizontal Air Flow Cooling

Horizontal air flow (HAF) cooling system uses small horizontal fans for moving the air mass and is considered to be an alternative to convection tube for the air distribution. In this method, the greenhouse may be visualized as a large box containing air, and fans located strategically moves the air in a circular pattern (Fig. 4.4). This system should move air at 0.6 to 0.9 $m^3/min/m^2$ of the greenhouse floor area. Fractional horsepower fans of 31 to 62 W (1/30 to 1115 hp) with a blade diameter of 41 cm (16 in) are sufficient for operation. The fans should be arranged in such a way that air flow is directed along the length of the greenhouse and parallel to the ground. The fans are placed at 0.6 to 0.9 m (2 to 3 ft) above plant height and at intervals of 15 m (50 ft). They are arranged such that the airflow is directed by one row of fans along the length of the greenhouse down one side to the opposite end and then back along the other side by another row of fans. Greenhouses of larger widths may require more number of rows of fans along its length.

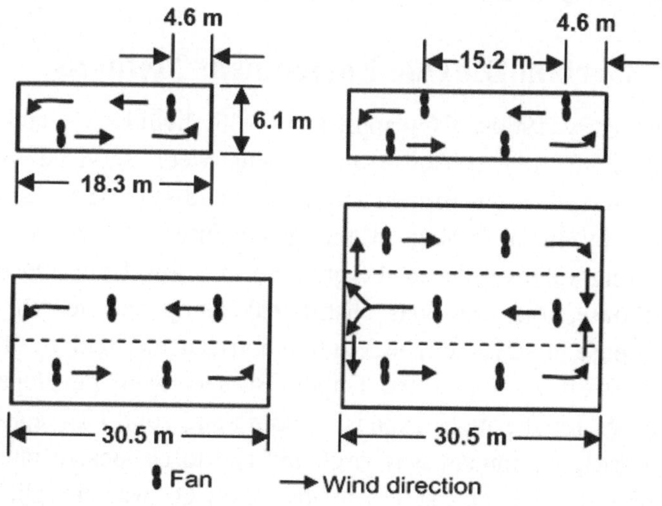

Fig. 4.4 Fan arrangements for HAF system in different sizes of greenhouses.

Temperatures at plant height are more uniform with the HAF system than with convection tube system. The HAF system makes use of the same exhaust fans, inlet louvers and controls as the convection tube system. The only difference is the use of HAF fans in the place of convection tubes for the air distribution. Cold air entering through the louvers located at the higher level in the gables of the greenhouse is drawn by the air circulation created by the network of HAF fans and to complete the cycle, proper quantity of air is let out through the exhaust fans. The combined action of louvered inlet, HAF fans and exhaust fans distribute the cold air throughout the greenhouse.

Similar to the convection tubes, the HAF fans can be used to distribute heat in the greenhouse. When neither cooling nor heating, is required, the HAF fans or convection tube can be used to bring warm air down from the upper level of the gable and to provide uniform temperature in the plant zone. It is possible to integrate summer and winter cooling systems with heating arrangements inside a greenhouse for the complete temperature control requirements for certain days of the season.

4.5 Carbon Dioxide Enrichment Methods

In the early 1960s, CO_2 applicators with liquid CO_2 tanks were installed at a greenhouse range and were serviced by CO_2 distributors. CO_2 gas formed above the liquid in these tanks and was carried by metal tubing to the greenhouses. A set of pressure regulating valves reduced the pressure to a low level. Once in the greenhouse, the gas was distributed along the length of the greenhouse in a plastic tube 3 to 6 mm in diameter with needle holes at every 30 cm along the length. Burners were developed as a substitute for the more expensive liquid and solid CO_2 applicators. Some early equipment was large and had to be located outside the greenhouse. The exhaust, essentially pure CO_2, was brought into the greenhouse through a duct and distributed along the length of the greenhouse. Smaller generators were developed that were installed overhead in the greenhouse. These systems are less expensive and they produce CO_2 in open-flame burners using kerosene, propane, or natural gas. Partly because of the recent shifts in fuel costs, larger greenhouse firms find the cost of CO_2 from direct sources of CO_2 comparable to that of CO_2 generated from the combustion of fuel. Unlike CO_2 generation in burners, the use of liquid CO_2 is of purity and releases no heat, which can be a disadvantage during the winter and advantage at the beginning and end of the hotter CO_2 injection season.

The simpler forms of CO_2 injection control use either a time clock or a light sensor to turn the CO_2 generator ON in the morning and OFF in the evening. During the day, the CO_2 generator is automatically turned OFF when the ventilating fans are ON. In the event of roof ventilation, mechanical switches are installed on the ventilators to allow the CO_2 generator to operate only when the vents are open less than 5 cm. Simple CO_2 testers consist of a small hand pump that is stroked a given number of times to pass air through a tube. The tube contains a CO_2 sensitive chemical that changes colour as CO_2 is absorbed. 'The length of the tube that changes colour is measured on a scale that directly indicates the level of CO_2 in the air passed through the tube.

The present, more sophisticated CO_2 generator control systems are based on CO_2 sensors. These sensors continually monitor the CO_2 level in the greenhouse and a single sensor can be connected to several greenhouses by sampling tubes and air samples drawn by a pump. The signal from the sensor is used to control the CO_2 generator so that a constant CO_2 level can be maintained. Information from the single sensor with multiple sampling tubes is received by a computer, which in turn controls CO_2 generators in each greenhouse.

REVIEW QUESTIONS

1. What are the different stages of evolution in control of greenhouse environment?
2. List the benefits of well controlled greenhouse environment.
3. What are the features of manual controlling?
4. Write a note on thermostats and the various types of sensors used in automatic control of temperature?
5. Explain the need for cooling the greenhouse in the summer and winter.

6. Describe the working of fan-and-pad cooling system with a neat sketch.
7. Explain the principle of working of fog cooling system and describe its features.
8. Describe the working of convection tube cooling system with a neat diagram.
9. Explain the working principle of HAF fan cooling system.
10. Draw layout diagrams of fan arrangements of HAF cooling system for different sizes of greenhouse.
11. Give a short note on the different methods of carbon dioxide enrichment, carbon dioxide measurement techniques and control.

Chapter 5

GREENHOUSE VENTILATION AND COMPUTERIZED CONTROL SYSTEMS

Ventilation is the process of allowing the fresh air to enter into the enclosed area by driving out the air with undesirable properties. In the greenhouse context, ventilation is essential for reducing temperature, replenishing CO_2 and controlling relative humidity. Ventilation requirements for greenhouses vary greatly, depending on the crop grown and the season of production. The ventilation system can be either a passive system (natural ventilation) or an active system (forced ventilation) using fans. Usually greenhouses that are used seasonally employ natural ventilation only. The plant response to specific environment factor is related to the physiological processes and hence the latter affects the yield and quality. Hence controlling of environment is of great importance to realize the complete benefits of CEA. Manual maintenance of uniform environmental conditions inside the greenhouse is very difficult and cumbersome. A poor maintenance results in less crop production, low quality and low income. For effective control, automatic control systems like microprocessor and computer are used presently to maintain the environment. Automatic control systems sense and measure the environmental parameters, compare it to a standard and, if needed, activate proper device which alters the parameter, to bring the measured parameter to the required level into agreements with the standard. This chapter deals with various features of natural ventilation, forced ventilation, microprocessors and computers in greenhouses.

5.1 Natural Ventilation

In the tropics, the sides of greenhouse structures are often left open for natural ventilation. Tropical greenhouse is primarily a rain shelter, a cover of polyethylene over the crop to prevent rainfall from entering the growing area. This mitigates the problem of foliage diseases, as some of the disease-causing pathogens require free water on plant foliage for development. With the advent of plastics and its use in greenhouses, provision of passive or natural ventilation is a challenge, especially in the absence of exhaust fans. In natural ventilation, the heated air becomes less dense and rises up. This warm air moves out and allows the dense cool air to flow into the greenhouse. Prevailing winds above certain level also aid in the creation of additional natural ventilation. Until 1950, all greenhouses were cooled by passive air movement through ventilators. Ventilators were located on both roof slopes adjacent to the ridge and also on, both side walls of the greenhouse. The ventilators on the roof as well as those on the side were of area, each about 10% of the total roof area. During winter cooling phase, the south roof ventilator was opened in stages to meet cooling needs. When greater cooling was required, the north ventilator was opened in addition to the south ventilator. In summer cooling phase, the south ventilator was opened first, followed by the north ventilator. Cool air entered through the side ventilators. As the incoming air moved across the greenhouse, it was warmed by sunlight and by mixing with the warmer greenhouse air. With the increase in temperature, the incoming air becomes lighter and rises up and flows out through the roof ventilators. This sets up a chimney effect, which in turn draws in more air from the side ventilators creating a continuous cycle (Fig. 5.1). This system did not adequately cool the greenhouse. On hot days, the interior walls and floor were frequently injected with water to help cooling.

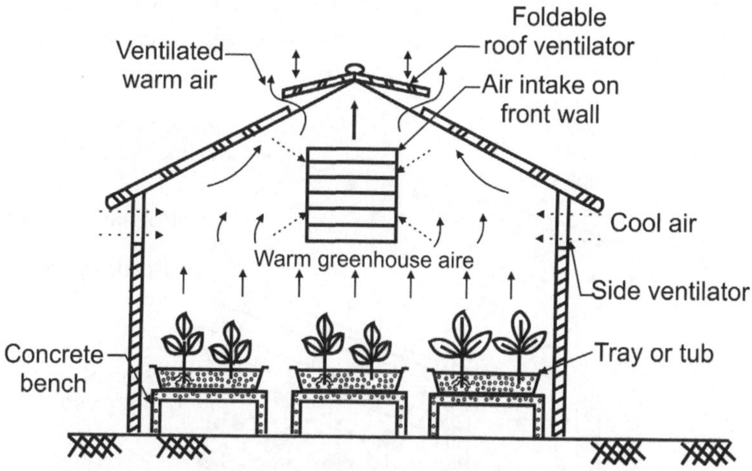

Fig. 5.1 Chimney effect in general passive ventilation.

Another method of ventilation is to roll up the sides, allowing air to flow across the plants (Fig. 5.2). The amount of ventilation on one side, or both sides, may be easily adjusted in response to temperature, prevailing wind and rain. During periods of excessive heat, it may be necessary to roll the sides up almost to the top. Passive ventilation can also be accomplished by manually raising or parting the polyethylene sheet. If insects, especially those that are vectors for virus diseases, are prevalent the open vent areas must be covered with screens. The holes must be large enough to permit free flow of air. Screens with small holes blocks air movement and cause a build up of dust. Such ventilation systems on plastic greenhouses are only effective on free standing greenhouses and not on gutter-connected greenhouses. Gutter-connected greenhouses are 8 m wide shelter type structures specially designed to utilize natural airflow for cooling. A new concept in natural ventilation for quonset greenhouses incorporates a 1 m continuous vent into the roof along the entire length of a gutter-connected greenhouse. The vent can be operated with a modernized vent thermostat for automatic climate control or by a computer system. In some designs, the whole roof is retractable (Fig. 5.3). The purpose of the side curtain and roof ventilator system or the retractable roof is to replace high energy consuming fan and pad cooling systems. These passive cooling systems work well in hot and cold climates, but the main limitation is the tolerance of the crop to full light intensity when the roof is opened.

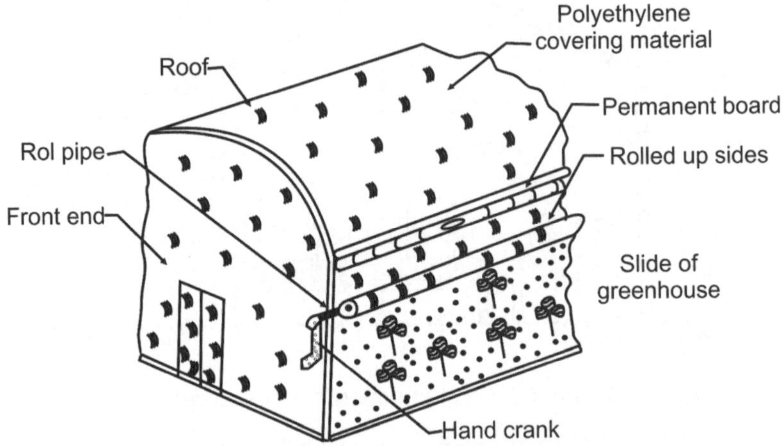

Fig. 5.2 Roll up side passive ventilation in polyhouse.

Fig. 5.3 Gutter-connected retractable roof polyethylene greenhouse.

5.2 Forced Ventilation

In forced or active ventilation, mechanical devices such as fans are used to expel the air. This type of ventilation can achieve uniform cooling. Forced ventilation system includes summer fan-and-pad and fog cooling systems, and the winter convection tube and horizontal airflow systems. For mechanical ventilation, low pressure, medium volume propeller blade fans, both directly connected and belt driven, are used for greenhouse ventilation. They are placed at the end of the greenhouse opposite to the air intake, which is normally covered by gravity or motorized louvers. The fan vents, or louvers, should be motorized, with their action controlled by fan operation. Motorized louvers prevent the wind from opening the louvers, especially when heat is being supplied to the greenhouse. Wall vents should be placed continuously across the end of the greenhouse to avoid hot areas in the crop zone.

Evaporative cooling in combination with fans is called as fan-and-pad cooling system. The fans and pads are usually arranged on opposite walls of the greenhouse (Fig. 5.4). The common types of cooling pads are made of excelsior (wood fiber), aluminium fiber, glass fiber, plastic fiber and cross-fluted cellulose material. Evaporative cooling systems are especially efficient in low humidity environments. There is growing interest in building greenhouses combining both passive (natural) and active (forced) systems of ventilation. Passive ventilation is utilized as the first stage of cooling, and the fan-pad evaporative cooling takes over when the passive system is not providing the needed cooling. At this stage, the vents for natural ventilation are closed. When both options for cooling are designed in greenhouse construction, the initial costs of installation will be more. But the operational costs are minimized in the long run, since natural ventilation will, most often meet the needed ventilation requirements.

Fogging systems is an alternative to evaporative pad cooling. They depend on absolutely clean water, free of any soluble salts, in order to prevent clogging of the mist nozzles. Such cooling systems are not as common as evaporative cooling pads, but when they become more cost competitive, they will be adopted widely. Fogging systems are the second stage of cooling, when passive systems are inadequate.

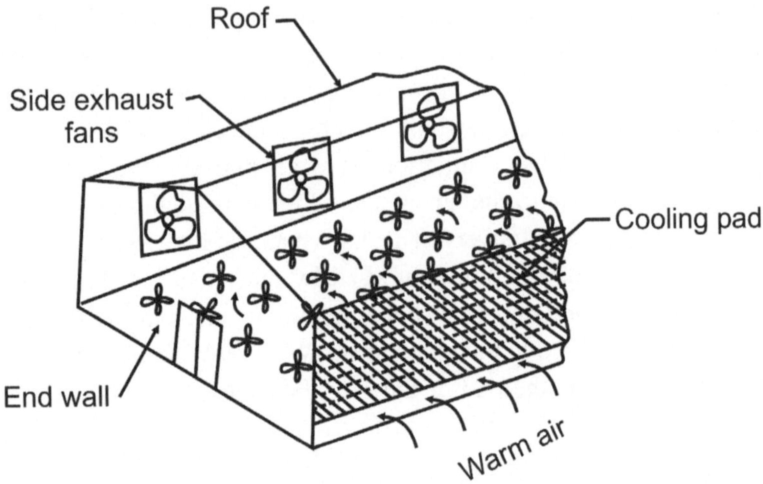

Fig. 5.4 Fan-and-pad type active summer cooling system.

5.3 Microprocessors

Dedicated microprocessors can be considered as simple computers. A typical microprocessor will have a keypad and a two or three line liquid crystal display of, sometimes, 80-character length for programming (Fig. 5.5). They generally do not have a floppy disk drive. They have more output connections and can control up to 20 devices. With this number of devices, it is cheaper to use a microprocessor. They can receive signals of several types, such as, temperature, light intensity, rain and wind speed. They permit integration of a diverse range of devices, which is not possible with thermostats. The accuracy of a microprocessor for temperature control is quite good. Unlike a thermostat, which is limited to a bimetallic strip or metallic tube for temperature sensing and its mechanical displacement for activation, the microprocessor often uses a thermistor. The bimetallic strip sensor has less reproducibility and a greater range between the ON and OFF steps. Microprocessors can be made to operate various devices, for instance, a microprocessor can operate the ventilators based on the information from the sensor for the wind direction and speed. Similarly a rain sensor can also activate the ventilators to prevent the moisture sensitive crop from getting wet. A microprocessor can be set to activate the CO_2 generator when the light intensity exceeds a given set point, a minimum level for photosynthesis.

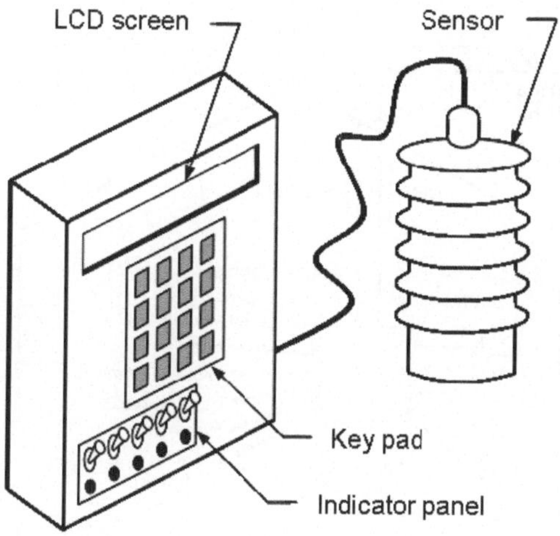

Fig. 5.5 Dedicated microprocessor for controlling greenhouse environment.

5.4 Computers

Now-a-days, computer control systems are common in greenhouse installation throughout Europe, Japan and the United States. Computer systems can provide fully integrated control of temperature, humidity, irrigation and fertilization, CO_2, light and shade levels for virtually any size growing facility. Precise control over a growing operation enables growers to realize savings of 15 to 50% in energy, water, chemical and pesticide applications. Computer controls normally help to achieve greater plant consistency, on-schedule production, higher overall plant quality and environmental purity.

A computer can control hundreds of devices (vents, heaters, fans, hot water mixing valves, irrigation valves, curtains and lights) within a greenhouse by utilizing dozens of input parameters, such as outside and inside temperatures, humidity, outside wind direction and velocity, CO_2 levels and even the time of day or night (Fig. 5.6).

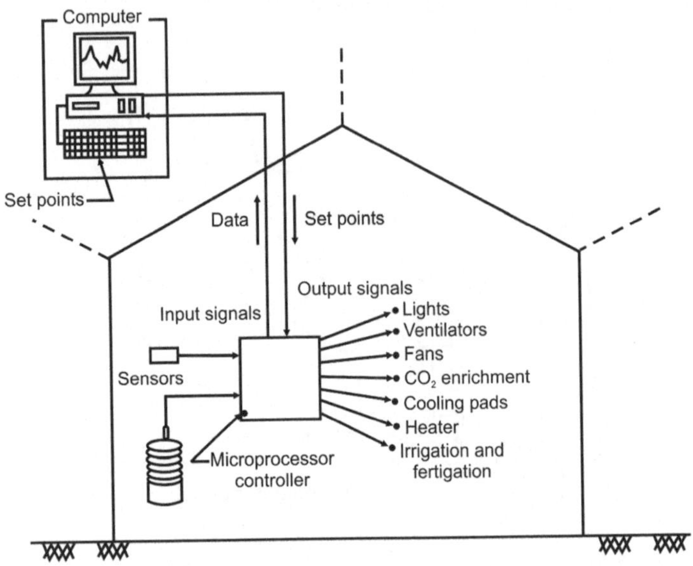

Fig. 5.6 Computerized control systems in greenhouse.

Computer systems receive signals from all sensors, evaluate all conditions and send appropriate commands at desired time intervals to each piece of equipment in the greenhouse range thus maintaining ideal conditions in each of the various independent greenhouse zones defined by the grower. Computers collect and record data provided by greenhouse production managers. Such a data acquisition system will enable the grower to gain a comprehensive knowledge of all factors affecting the quality and timeliness of the product.

A computer produces graphs of past and current environmental conditions both inside and outside the greenhouse complex. Using a data printout option, growers can produce reports and summaries of environmental conditions such as temperature, humidity and the CO_2 status for a given day, or over a longer period of time for current or later use.

As more environmental factors in the greenhouse are controlled, there comes a stage when individual controls cannot be coordinated to prevent system overlap. An example is the greenhouse thermostat calling for heating while the exhaust fans are still running. With proper software program, which uses the environmental parameters as input from different sensors, can effectively coordinate all the equipment without overlap and precisely control all parameters affecting plant development as desired. Despite the attraction of the computer systems, it should be remembered that the success of any production system is totally dependent on the grower's knowledge of the system and the crop management. Computers can only assist by adding precision to the overall greenhouse production practice, and they are only as effective as the software it runs and the efficiency of the operator.

5.4.1 Advantages of Computerized Control System

1. The computer always knows what all systems are doing and, if programmed properly, can coordinate these systems without overlap to provide the optimum environment.
2. The computer can record the environmental data, which can be displayed to show current conditions or stored and processed ones to provide a history of the cropping period, and if desired it may also be displayed in table or graph form.
3. A high-speed computer with networking facility can control several remotely located greenhouses, by placing the computer in a central area and the results can be monitored frequently by the management.
4. With proper programming and sensing systems, the computer can anticipate weather changes and make adjustments in heating and ventilation systems, thus saving energy.

5. The computer can be programmed to sound an alarm if conditions become unacceptable to and to detect sensor and equipment failure.

5.4.2 Disadvantages of Computerized Control System

1. High initial cost investment.
2. Requires qualified operators.
3. High maintenance, care and precautions are required.
4. Not economical for small scale and seasonal production.

REVIEW QUESTIONS

1. What is ventilation? Why it is required and what are the different types?
2. Explain chimney effect and describe the different methods of natural or passive ventilation of greenhouses with sketches.
3. Give a brief note on the methods of forced ventilation.
4. Bring out the features of microprocessors with a diagram that are used in greenhouse controls
5. Describe about the role of computers in controlling the greenhouse environment with a schematic diagram of greenhouse computerized control system.
6. Enumerate the advantages and disadvantages of computerized control system of controlling greenhouse environment.

Chapter 6

PLANNING OF GREENHOUSE FACILITY

A greenhouse has basically one purpose of providing and maintaining a growing environment that will result in optimum production at maximum yield. The agriculture in the controlled environment is possible in all the regions irrespective of climate and weather. As an enclosing structure for growing plants, greenhouse must admit the visible light portion of solar radiation for plant photosynthesis and, therefore, must be transparent. At the same time, to protect the plants, a greenhouse must be ventilated or cooled during the day because of the heat load from the radiation. The structure must also be heated or insulated during cold nights. A greenhouse acts as a barrier between the plant production areas and the external or ambient environment. Production is protected from external stresses such as weather and pollution from industrial and other sources. Hence, while planning for greenhouse facility care must be taken in the selection of site and its orientation, in choosing the type of structural design and in the choice of covering material for better functioning and operation of greenhouses. Various aspects of selection are planning of greenhouse facility are discussed in this chapter.

6.1 Site Selection and Orientation

A greenhouse is designed to withstand local wind, snow and crop loads for a specific cropping activity. In this way, the structure becomes location and crop specific. The building site should be as level as possible to reduce the cost of grading, and the site should be well aerated and should receive good solar radiation. Provision of a drainage system is always advisable, because of the extensive use of water in greenhouse operations. Where drainage is a problem, it is wise to install tile drainage below the surface prior to the construction of greenhouse. It is also advisable to select a site with a natural windbreak, such as a tree line or hill, on the north and northwest sides. In regions where snow is expected, trees should be 30.5 m away in order to keep drifts back from the greenhouses. To prevent shadows on the crop, trees located on the east, south, or west sides should be at a distance of 2.5 times their height. Owing to the limited availability of the agricultural labourers, high wages are to be paid to attract them. Higher wages can be offset by automation, which reduces the number of employees but increases productivity.

6.2 Structural Design

Many types of greenhouse structures are successfully employed in protected agriculture, and each type has its own advantages and is well suited for a particular case. The most important function of the greenhouse structure and its covering is the protection of the crop against hostile weather conditions (low and high temperatures, snow, hail, rain and wind), diseases and pests. It is important to develop greenhouses with a maximum intensity of natural light inside. The structural parts that can cast shadows in the greenhouse should be minimized. So the covering materials should have the largest possible unsupported area, and consequently offer the highest possible light transmittance. At the same time, greenhouse structures and structural components, including the covering, should be strong enough to resist loads from snow, wind, crops and installations, to provide adequate margins of safety to prevent structural damage or serviceability problems. A judicious component selection should be made since the light transmittance counteracts with the structural stability.

The different structural designs of greenhouse based on the types of frames are available (Fig. 6.1). A straight side wall and an arched roof (Fig. 6.1(a)) is possibly the most common shape for a greenhouse, but the gable roof (Fig. 6.1 (b)) is also widely used. Both structures can be free standing or gutter connected with the arch roof greenhouse. The arch roof and hoop style (Fig. 6.1(c)) greenhouses are most often constructed of galvanized iron pipe bent into form by a roller pipe bender. If tall growing crops are to be grown in a greenhouse or when benches are used, it is best to use a straight side wall structure (Fig. 6.1(d)) rather than a hoop style house, this ensures the best operational use of the greenhouse. A hoop type greenhouse is suitable for low growing crops, such as lettuce, or for nursery stock that are housed throughout the winter in greenhouses located in extremely cold regions. A Gothic arch frame structure (Fig. 6.1(e)) can be designed to provide adequate side wall height without loss of strength to the structure. This form of structure, along with others, can be used as a single free standing greenhouse or as a large range of multi-span, gutter connected units.

Loads to be considered while designing the greenhouse structures include the weight of the structure itself and, if supported by the structure, load of equipment for the heating and ventilation and water lines. The load may also include the weight of crops if they are trained to a support system carried by the greenhouse frame, and also loads from wind and snow. Greenhouse structures should be designed to resist a 130 km/h wind velocity. The actual load depends on wind angle, greenhouse shape and size, and the presence or absence of openings and wind breaks. The ultimate design of a greenhouse consists of a balance of the following aspects:

1. Overall structural design and the properties of the individual structural components.

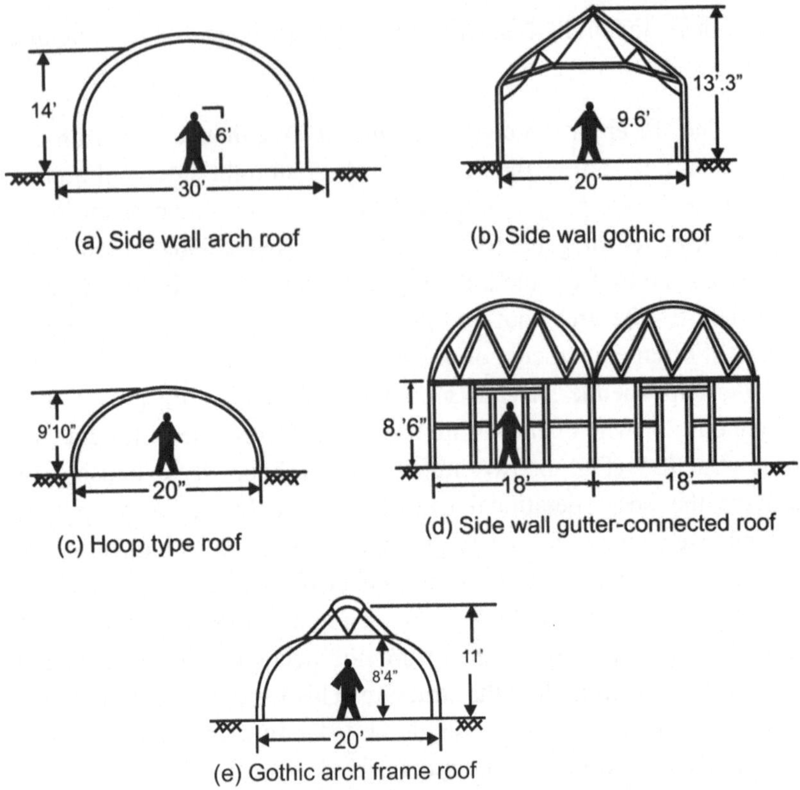

Fig. 6.1 Structural designs of different greenhouse frameworks.

2. Specific mechanical and physical properties, which determine the structural behaviour of the covering materials.
3. Specific sensitivity of the crop to light and temperature to be grown in the greenhouse.
4. Specific requirements relevant to the physical properties of the covering material.
5. Agronomic requirements of the crop.

6.3 Covering Materials

The factors to be considered while selecting the greenhouse covering material are light transmission, covering material weight, resistance to impact, durability to outdoor weathering and thermal stability over wide range of temperatures. The purpose for which the greenhouse facility is intended determines the selection of a covering material. For example, in temperate regions where high temperatures are required, the covering material with high light transmission and far IR absorption must be selected. Also the loss of heat by conduction should be minimized. Another important aspect in selection of covering material is the service life of material. A well maintained glass and acrylic sheet can last for many years, even up to 20 years or more. The polycarbonate and fiberglass-reinforced polyester sheet has a service life of 5 to 12 years. Of all the covering materials, polyethylene has the least service life of 2 to 6 months only, but when the film is stabilized for UV rays, the life is extended to two to three years.

The following are the properties of an ideal greenhouse selective covering material:

1. It should transmit the visible light portion of the solar radiation, which is utilized by plants for photosynthesis.
2. It should absorb the small amount of UV in the radiation and convert a portion of it to fluoresce into visible light, useful for plants.
3. It should reflect or absorb IR radiation which are not useful to plants and causes greenhouse interiors to overheat.
4. It should be of low cost.
5. It should have usable life of 10 to 20 years.

Such a covering material will obviously improve CEA performance, reducing solar heat load, increasing light levels and crop yields.

REVIEW QUESTIONS

1. What are the factors to be considered in site selection and orientation of greenhouses?

2. Write about the structural designs of different greenhouse frame works with neat sketches.
3. Give a note on the factors to be considered while selecting the covering material.
4. List the features of an ideal greenhouse selective covering material.

Chapter 7

GREENHOUSE CONSTRUCTION MATERIALS

Materials that are commonly used to build frames for greenhouses are wood, bamboo, steel, galvanized iron pipe, aluminium and reinforced concrete. Frames often incorporate a combination and alloys of these materials. The selection of these materials was based on their specific physical properties and requirements of design strength. Life expectancy and the cost of the construction materials also decide the selection of materials. The general characteristics of the materials of greenhouse construction, such as wood, galvanized iron and glass and their suitability in specific components of construction are discussed in this chapter.

7. 1 Wood

Wood and bamboo are generally used for low cost polyhouses. In these houses, the wood is used for making frames consisting of side posts and columns over which the polyethylene sheet is fixed (Fig. 7.1). The commonly used woods are pine and casuarina, which are strong and less expensive. In pipe-framed polyhouses, wooden battens can be used in the end frames for fixing the covering material. In tropical areas, bamboo is often used to form the gable roof of a greenhouse structure. Wood must be painted white to improve light conditions within the greenhouse, but care should be taken to select a paint that will inhibit the growth of mold. Wood must also be treated for protection against decay. Special treatment should be given to the wood that may come into contact with the soil. Chromated copper arsenate and ammonical copper arsenate are water based preservatives that are safe to use where plants are grown. Even natural decay resistance woods, such as redwood or cypress should be treated, in desert or tropical regions, but they are expensive.

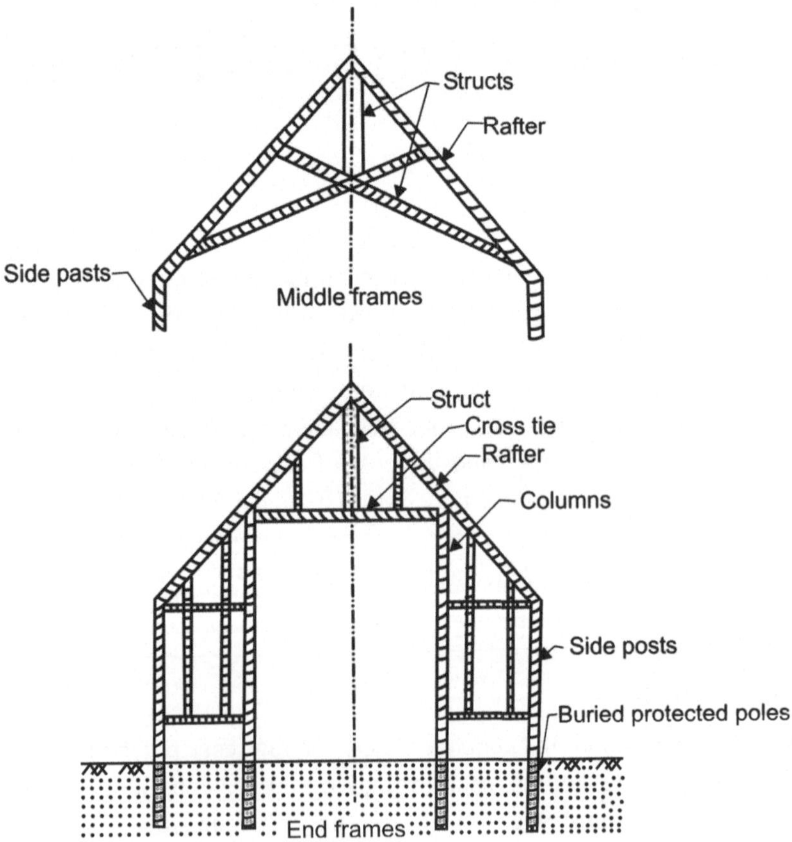

Fig. 7.1 Wooden scissors-truss type film plastic greenhouse.

7.2 Galvanized Iron, Aluminium, Steel and Reinforced Cement Concrete

Galvanized iron (GI) and steel members are generally used in different frame works of greenhouse structure designs. In galvanizing operation the surface of iron or steel is coated with a thin layer of zinc to protect it against corrosion. Among many others, the two commonly followed processes are:

1. Hot dip galvanizing (hot process) where the cleaned member is dipped in molten zinc, which produces a skin of zinc alloy to the steel.
2. Electro-galvanizing (cold process) where the member is zinc plated similar to the process of electro-plating.

As the wood is becoming scarce and more expensive, GI pipes, tubular steel and angle iron are used for side posts, columns and purlins. The galvanization process makes the iron rust proof; hence the common problem of rusting of iron structural members is eliminated. In the pipe frames, GI pipes are mostly used as side posts, columns, cross ties and purlins. All the pipe components are not interconnected but depend on the attachment to the sash bars for support.

Often the frames may be all aluminium or steel or a combination of the two materials. Aluminium and hot dipped GI are comparatively maintenance free. In tropical areas, it is advisable to double dip the steel, especially when the single dip galvanizing process does not give a complete zinc cover of even thickness to the steel. Aluminium and steel must be protected from direct contact with the ground to prevent corrosion. If there is a risk of any part of the aluminium or steel coming into contact with the ground it must be thoroughly painted with bitumen tar.

For truss frames, flat steel, tubular steel or angle iron is welded together to form a truss consisting of rafters, chords and struts. The angle iron purlins running throughout the length of the greenhouses are bolted to each truss. Now-a-days, the greenhouse construction is of metal type that is more permanent.

While use of reinforced cement concrete is generally limited to foundations and low walls, concrete is sometimes used as support posts for frames made of bamboo. In permanent bigger greenhouses, floors and benches for growing the crops are also made of concrete.

7.3 Glass

Glass has been the traditional glazing material all over the world. The most widely used glass for greenhouse is the "single drawn" or "float glass", secondly the "hammered" and "tempered glass". Single drawn glass is made in the traditional way by simply pulling the molten glass either by hand or by mechanical equipment. Float glass is made in modern way by allowing the molten glass to float on the molten tin. The single drawn or float glass has a uniform thickness of 3 to 4 mm. The term "hammered glass" defines a cast glass with one face (exterior) smooth and the other one (interior) rough, designed so as to enhance light diffusion. Therefore, this glass is not transparent but translucent. The thickness of this type of glass is usually 4 mm. The tempered glass is the glass, which is quickly cooled after manufacture, adopting a procedure similar to that used for steel. This kind of processing gives the glass higher resistance to impact which is generally caused by hail. Coatings for glass, such as metal oxide with a low emissivity are used for saving of energy with adequate light transmittance. Such coatings are applied only to float glasses.

Glass though fragile, is a strong material when it is used properly and loaded in the correct way. Glass, used as a covering material of greenhouses, is expected to be subjected to rather severe wind loading, snow and hail loading conditions. To limit the chances of breakage of glass coverings, design rules should be applied to the supporting structure of the glass panels. Such rules are aimed, in general, at limiting the deformation of the structural components which are supporting the glass panels. Thus, the standard properties of the glass to be used as construction material are as follows

(Briassoulis, et al, 1997). The maximum bending deflection (u_{gut}) of gutters, purlins in the roof and ridge profiles is given by:

$$u_{gut} \leq \frac{L_{trs}}{650-100n} \leq \frac{L_{trs}}{250} \leq 18 \text{ mm}$$

where, L_{trs} is the distance between trusses and n is the number of panels within this distance.

The maximum bending deflection (u_{gab}) of gable supporting parts is given by:

$$u_{gab} \leq \frac{L_{gab}}{150} \leq 25\text{mm}$$

where, L_{gab} is the length of gable column or gable purlin.

The maximum bending deflection (u_{gla}) of glazing bars for support of rigid materials is given by:

$$u_{gla} \leq \frac{L_{gla}}{100} \leq 20\text{mm}$$

where, L_{gla} is the span of the glazing bar.

Also, to provide the proper supporting conditions for glass panels, rules are given for the grooves in glazing bars. Different calculation methods are given for glass panels depending on whether they are supported on 2, 3 or 4 sides. The strength mainly depends on the length/width ratio of the panel and on the thickness of the panel, but the most widely used thickness is 4 mm.

REVIEW QUESTIONS

1. How wood can be utilized as a construction material of greenhouse?

2. Give the diagram of the middle and end frames of the wooden scissors-truss type film plastic greenhouse and label the components.

3. Write short notes on the following constructional materials of greenhouse:

   (a) Galvanized iron

   (b) Aluminium

   (c) Steel

   (d) Reinforced cement concrete

4. Describe the different types of glasses used as greenhouse covering material and give the rules of fixing it based on the deflection.

Chapter 8

GREENHOUSE COVERING MATERIALS

Flexible plastic films, including polyethylene, polyester and polyvinyl chloride, have been used for greenhouse coverings. Polyethylene is principally used today for two reasons. Firstly, film plastic greenhouses with permanent metal frames cost less than glass greenhouses. Even greater savings can be realized when film plastic is applied to less permanent frames, such as quonset greenhouses. Secondly, film plastic greenhouses are popular because the cost of heating them is approximately 40% lower compared to single-layer glass or fiberglass-reinforced plastic greenhouses. A thermal screen is installed inside a glass greenhouse that will lower the heat requirement to approximately that of a double-layer film plastic greenhouse, but this increases the cost of the glass greenhouse. Polyethylene film was developed in the late 1930s in England, and its use as a greenhouse covering was pioneered around the middle of this century. The use of polyethylene for greenhouses has increased rapidly and continues to do so.

Some disadvantages exist along with the advantages of film plastic. These covering materials are short lived compared to glass and plastic panels. UV light from the sun causes the plastic to darken, thereby lowering transmission of light, also making it brittle, which leads to its breakage due to wind. However, under proper management, the savings in fuel as well as the lower initial purchase price make the film plastic greenhouse less costly than a glass greenhouse. In this chapter, salient features of greenhouse covering films, such as polyethylene, polyvinyl chloride, polyester, Tefzel T^2 and rigid panels like fiberglass-reinforced plastic, polycarbonate are discussed.

8.1 Polyethylene Film

From the large variety of plastics available today in the market, those commonly used for greenhouse coverings are the thermoplastics. The basic characteristic of thermoplastics is that they consist of individual long chain molecules. They soften with heating and harden with cooling and this process is reversible. Thermoplastics constitute a group of materials that are attractive to the designer for two main reasons:

1. Their basic physical properties can be exploited in a wide range of properly designed articles that have the stiffness, robustness and resilience to resist loads and deformations imposed during normal use.
2. They can readily be processed using efficient mass production techniques which result in low labour charge.

Polyethylenes used for covering year-round production greenhouses have a UV-inhibitor in it. Otherwise, it lasts for only one heating season. UV-grade polyethylene is available in widths up to 15.2 m in flat sheets and up to 7.6 m in tubes. Standard lengths include 30.5, 33.5, 45.7, 61.0 and 67.0 m. Several companies provide custom lengths up to a maximum of 91.5 m. A polyethylene covering is colder than the air inside the greenhouse during winter. When warm and moist greenhouse air comes in contact with the cold polyethylene, the air gets cooled. As a result, water vapour condenses on the polyethylene surface. Since the surface is repellent to water, the water forms into beads and with time the water beads increase in size to a point where they drop off to the plants below.

The wet foliage fosters disease development, while the constantly wetted soil becomes waterlogged and oxygen deficient. With the antifog surfactant (a chemical discouraging condensation) built into the film or panel, it is advisable to use them because in addition to the water dripping problems, this condensation also reduces light intensity within the greenhouse. Warm objects, such as plants, the greenhouse frame and soil radiate IR energy to colder bodies, such as the sky at night. This condition results in loss of heat in greenhouses. Since polyethylene is a poor barrier to radiant heat, polyethylene formulated with IR-blocking chemicals into it during manufacture will stop about half of the radiant heat loss. On cold and clear nights, as much as 25% of the total heat loss of a greenhouse can be prevented in this way and on cloudy nights only 15% is prevented.

UV-stabilized polyethylene, on an average, transmits about 87% of photosynthetically active radiation (PAR) into the greenhouse. IR-absorbing polyethylene, which reduces radiant heat loss, transmits about 82% of PAR. The amount of light passing through two layers of a greenhouse covering is approximately the square of the decimal fraction of the amount passing through one layer. For instance, when 87% passes through one layer of UV-inhibited polyethylene, only 76% (0.87 × 0.87) passes through two layers. Similarly, PAR transmission through two layers of IR-absorbing polyethylene, each having 82% transmittance, is 67%. When the structure is not in use, the plastic may be removed to prevent unnecessary degradation by UV light. If this is done, an UV-inhibited plastic cover may last for a period of four to five years.

8.2 Polyvinyl Chloride Film

Polyvinyl chloride films are UV light resistant vinyl films of 0.2 and 0.3 mm (8 and 12 mil) thicknesses (1 mil = 1/1000 in) and are guaranteed for four and five years respectively. This extended life period was a definite advantage in the recent past, when polyethylene lasted for only one or two years. With the recent advent of four-year polyethylene, this advantage is nearly gone. The cost of 0.3 mm (12 mil) vinyl is three times that of 0.15 mm (6 mil) polyethylene.

Although vinyl film is produced in rolls up to 1.27 m wide, any width strip can be purchased, since the strips of vinyl can be sealed together. The vinyl films tend to hold a static electrical charge, which attracts and holds dust. This in turn reduces light transmittance unless the dust is washed off. Vinyl films are seldom used in the United States. In Japan, 95% of greenhouses are covered with film plastic and within this group 90% are covered with vinyl film.

8.3 Polyester Film

Polyester films offer long life and are strong. Films of 0.13 mm (5 mil) thickness are used for roofs and will last for four years, while 0.08 mm (3 mil) films are used on vertical walls and have a life expectancy of seven years. Although the cost of polyester is higher than that of polyethylene, it was offset by the extra life expectancy. Other advantages include light transmittance equal to that of glass and freedom from static electrical charges, which collect dust. Polyester is still used frequently, in heat retention screens because of its high capacity to block radiant energy.

8.4 Tefzel T^2 Film

The most recent addition of greenhouse film plastic covering is Tefzel T^2 film (ethylene tetrafluoroethylene). Actually, this film was earlier used as the transparent covering on solar collectors. The anticipated life expectancy is 20 years or more. The light transmission is 95% and is greater than that of any other greenhouse covering material. A double layer has a light transmission of 90% (0.95×0.95). Tefzel T^2 film is more transparent to IR radiation than other film plastics. Hence less heat is trapped inside the greenhouse during hot weather. As a result less cooling energy is required. On the negative side, the film is available only in 1.27 m wide rolls. This requires clamping rails on the greenhouse for every 1.2 m. Efforts are underway to produce wider sheets of the film. If reasonable width strips become available, the price will not be excessive because a double layer covering will still cost less than a polycarbonate panel covering with its aluminium extrusions, and will last longer, and will have much higher light intensity inside the greenhouse.

8.5 Polyvinyl Chloride Rigid-Panel

Initially, polyvinyl chloride (PVC) rigid panels showed promise as an inexpensive covering material (about 40% of cost of fiberglass reinforced plastics). They had a life expectancy of five years or more, when polyethylene lasted one year. Commercial use of these panels soon indicated that this life expectancy was much short, sometimes as little as two years. This was unacceptable as the cost of PVC panels was four to five times that of polyethylene film and they required much more time to install. Now-a-days, PVC rigid panels are not in use.

8.6 Fiberglass-Reinforced Plastic Rigid Panel

Fiberglass-reinforced plastic (FRP) was more popular as a greenhouse covering material in the recent past (Fig. 8.1). Based on the grade, the usable life period of FRP panel varies. Some grades give five to ten years while better grades can last up to 20 years. Corrugated panels were used because of their greater strength. Flat panels are occasionally used for the end and side walls where the load is not great. Panels are available in 1.3 m widths, lengths up to 7.3 m, and in a variety of colours. The panels are flexible enough to conform to the shape of quonset greenhouses, which make FRP a very versatile covering material. FRP panels can be applied to the inexpensive frames of film plastic greenhouses or to the more elaborate frames of glass type greenhouses. In the former case, the price of the FRP panel greenhouse lies between that of a film plastic greenhouse and that of a glass greenhouse, but the cost is compensated by the elimination of the need for replacement of film plastic. In the latter case, the FRP panel greenhouse costs about the same as the glass greenhouse.

Fig. 8.1 Fiberglass-reinforced plastic rigid panel greenhouse.

The advantage of FRP panel is that it is more resistant to breakage by factors, such as hail or vandals. Sunlight passing through FRP is scattered by the fibers in the panels, with the result that light intensity is rather uniform throughout the greenhouse in comparison with a glass covering. Disadvantage of FRP panels is that they are subjected to etching and pitting by dust abrasion and chemical pollution. The total quantity of light transmitted through clear FRP is approximately equivalent to that transmitted through glass but diminishes in relation to its colour. For greenhouse crops, in general, only clear FRP permits a satisfactory level of light transmission (88 to 90%). Coloured FRP panels has found a limited use in greenhouses intended for growing houseplants that require low light intensity, and in display greenhouses used for holding plants during the sales period. Also, FRP has the distinct advantage over glass that it cools easily. FRP panel greenhouses require fewer structural members since sash bars are not needed.

8.7 Acrylic and Polycarbonate Rigid Panel

Acrylic and poly carbonate double-layer rigid panels have been available for about 15 years for greenhouse use. The panels have been used for glazing the side and end walls of film plastic greenhouses and for retrofitting old glass greenhouse, while the acrylic panels are highly inflammable, the polycarbonate panels are non flammable. The acrylic panels are popular due to their higher light transmission and longer life. Polycarbonate panels are preferred for commercial greenhouses due to lower price, flame resistance, and greater resistance to hail damage. Acrylic panels are available in thicknesses of 16 and 18 mm, and have 83% of PAR light transmission. The thicker panels cannot be bent, but the thinner panels can be bent to fit curved-roof greenhouses. These panels are also available with a coating to prevent condensation drip. Polycarbonate panels are available in thicknesses of 4, 6, 8, 10 and 16 mm. These panels are also available with a coating to prevent condensation drip and also with an acrylic coating for extra protection from UV light.

REVIEW QUESTIONS

1. What are the reasons of popularity of flexible plastic films as greenhouse covering materials and the associated disadvantages?
2. Describe the features of polyethylene film and the various types of specialty films in the category.
3. Write short notes on the following covering material:
   (a) Polyvinyl chloride film
   (b) Polyester film
   (c) Tefzel T^2 film
4. Discuss about the fiberglass reinforced plastic rigid panel as the greenhouse covering material.
5. Give a brief note on acrylic and polycarbonate rigid panel used in greenhouse construction.

Chapter 9

CONSTRUCTION OF TYPICAL GREENHOUSES

The term greenhouse refers to a structure covered with a transparent material for the purpose of admitting natural light for plant growth. The structure is usually heated artificially and differs from other growing structures, such as cold frames and hotbeds, in that it is sufficiently high to permit a person to work from within. Quite frequently, two or more greenhouses in one location are referred to as a greenhouse range. A building associated with the greenhouses that is used for storage or for operations in support of growing of plants, but not as such used for growing plants, is referred to as a service building or headhouse. The choice of the greenhouse structure also depends on the covering material to be used.

A glass house requires heavier structure to support the weight of glass in addition to other external loads. Generally, a single design of greenhouse is popular under a very wide range of loads and crops. But greenhouse designs need to be modified in view of the specific construction, environmental control systems and crops. The greenhouse design must be energy conserving while maintaining adequate transparency to solar energy. Local climate and local materials must be taken into account to choose the most appropriate greenhouse design. This chapter describes in detail the basic design criteria of the greenhouse construction and specifically the construction procedures of glass greenhouse and pipe framed greenhouse.

9.1 Design Criteria of Construction

For locating the greenhouse a piece of land larger than the grower's immediate needs should be acquired. The ultimate size of the greenhouse range should be estimated. Area should then be added to this estimated figure to accommodate service buildings, storage, access drives and a parking lot. Doubling the area covered by greenhouses will give a bare minimum land requirement, which will include unforeseen needs. The floor area of service buildings required for small firms is about 13% of the greenhouse floor area, and it decreases with the increase in size of the firm. On an average, service buildings occupy 10% of the growing area. The different aspects of greenhouse site selection and orientation should be considered while designing for the facility.

It is important to develop a greenhouse floor plan that allows for an efficient operation. Floor plans can be made to allow for additions to the service building and greenhouses without removal of previous buildings or the addition of multiple service buildings (Fig. 9.1). The service building is centrally located in a nearly square design of the firm, which minimizes distances of movement of plants and materials. When future expansion works are carried out, the walls of adjacent greenhouses or service buildings between each building phase are removed. Doors between the service building and the greenhouse should be wide enough to facilitate full use of the corridor width. Doors at least 3.1 m wide and 2.7 m high are common. It is good to have the greenhouse gutter at least 3.7 m above the floor to accommodate automation and thermal blanket and still leave room for future innovations. Service buildings are constructed from a variety of materials, buildings with steel members being the most common. Usually economy determines the type of greenhouse to be constructed. Some growers use a few bays of the greenhouse itself for the service building operations. This design lowers the cost by 25 to 50%.

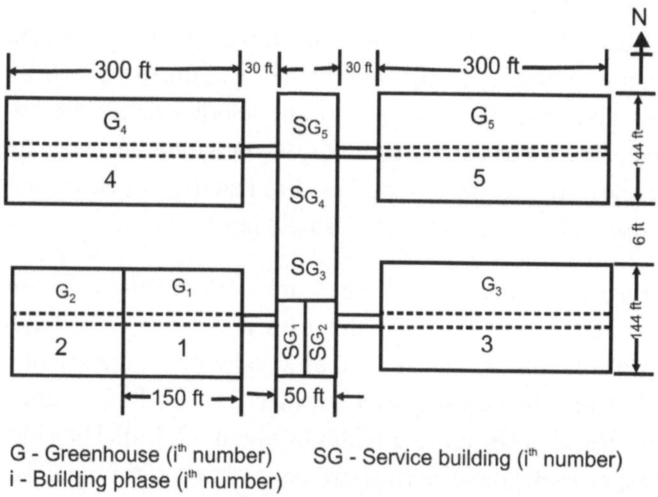

Fig. 9.1 Floor plan for a greenhouse firm showing construction in phases.

9.2 Construction of Glass Greenhouses

Glass greenhouses have an advantage of greater interior light intensity over plastic panel and film plastic covered greenhouses. Glass greenhouses tend to have a higher air infiltration rate, which leads to lower interior humidity, which is advantageous for disease prevention. On the other hand, glass greenhouses have a higher initial cost than double-layer film plastic greenhouses. While comparing the price of a glass greenhouse to a film plastic greenhouse, one needs to take into account the initial purchase price of each as well as the cost of re-covering the film plastic greenhouse every three to four years.

Several types of glass greenhouses are designed to meet specific needs. A lean-to design is used when a greenhouse is placed against the side of an existing building. This design makes the best use of sunlight and minimizes the requirements for roof supports. It is found mostly in the retail industry. An even-span greenhouse is one in which the two roof slopes are of equal pitch and width. By comparison, an uneven-span greenhouse has roofs of unequal width, which make the structure adaptable to the side of a hill. This style is seldom used today because such greenhouses are not adaptable to automation. Finally, a ridge-and-furrow design uses, two or more A-frame greenhouses connected to one another along the length of the eave. The eave serves as a furrow or gutter to carry rain and melted snow away. The sidewall is eliminated between greenhouses, which results in a structure with a single large interior.

Basically, three frame types are used in glass greenhouses. Wood frames are used for greenhouses under 6.1 m in width. Side posts and columns are constructed of wood without the use of a truss, whereas wider houses required sturdier frames. Pipe frames serve well for greenhouses up to a width of about 12.2 m. The side posts, columns, cross ties and purlins are constructed from pipe. The pipe components are not all interconnected but depend on attachment to the sash bars for support. Some greenhouses less than 15.2 m in width and most over this width are built on truss frames. Flat steel, tubular steel or angle iron is welded together to form a truss encompassing the rafters, chords and struts. Struts are support members under compression, while chords are support members under tension. Angle iron purlins running through the length of the greenhouse are bolted to each truss. A frame thus constructed can stand without support of sash bars. Columns are used only in very wide truss frame houses of about 21.3 m and wider. Latest glass greenhouses are primarily of the truss frame type. Truss frame greenhouses are best suited for prefabrication, which makes the construction of greenhouses more economical over the years. Automation is more efficient in wider houses, which require the strength of truss frames.

The glass on the greenhouse is attached to sash bars. In earlier days, sash bars were made exclusively of wood, primarily cypress and redwood. The wood required periodic painting to protect it against rot and it is costly. Aluminum sash bars and ventilators were introduced in the early 1950s. The consequent all-metal greenhouses are very expensive to invest but quickly became competitive with houses having wooden sash bars. All-metal greenhouses proved cheaper to maintain since they required no painting. At present, virtually all glass greenhouse construction is of the metal type. The structural members of the glass greenhouse cast shadows that reduce plant growth during the dark months of the year. Aluminum sash bars are stronger than wooden ones; hence wider panes of glass can be used with aluminum bars. The reduction in structural materials plus the reflectance of aluminum have given these metal greenhouses a great advantage over wooden greenhouses in terms of higher interior light intensity. Different types of glasses, such as double-strength float glass, tempered glass, hammered glass, low-iron and high light transmission glass were used in the construction of greenhouses.

Glass greenhouse construction of today can be categorized as high profile or low profile. The low profile greenhouse is most popular in the Netherlands and is known as the Venlo greenhouse. Eaves are 3.2 m apart and single panes of glass extend from eave to ridge. The lower profile slightly reduces exposed surface area, thereby reducing the heating cost. It is to be remembered, however, that these greenhouses are more expensive to cool when fans are required in warm climates. High profile greenhouses have greater eaves spacing and require more than single pane to cover the eave to the ridge. These greenhouses are available with special sash bars that hold two or even three layers of glass. This layering produces one or two dead air spaces to reduce heat loss. A problem with this design is the unsealed junction between pieces of glass in the inner layer. Moisture and dust may enter between the layers and reduce light transmission. It is expensive to remove and clean the glass.

9.3 Construction of Pipe Framed Greenhouses

In the prevailing economic conditions, where capital is a scarce input, the choice often favours low initial investment and relatively long life greenhouses. Structural members of galvanized mild steel pipe in combination with wide width UV-stabilized low density polyethylene (LDPE) film are preferred by greenhouse designers. A greenhouse structure has three distinct segments, namely, frame, cladding material and the environment control devices. All the three components have different designated life spans.

9.3.1 Material Requirement

The structural members of greenhouse are hoops, foundation, lateral supports, polygrip assembly and end frame. The end frames can be made of wood and other members are made of galvanized steel. The following are the materials required for a greenhouse having 4 m × 20 m floor area (Fig. 9.2): GI pipe class A (25 mm ϕ, 85 cm long, 30 m total length), GI pipe class B (15 mm ϕ, 6.0 m length, 21 Nos.), GI sheet (20 gauge, 90 × 24 cm, 4 sheets), mild steel (MS) flat (25 × 3mm, 4 m length), lateral support to end frames (10 mm ϕ rod, 10 m length), cement concrete (1:3:6 mix, 1.0 m^3), UV-stabilized LDPE film (single layer, 800 gauge, 5.4 m^2/kg, 154 m^2), poly grip (channel 2000 × 3.5 × 4 cm, 2 Nos. and angle 2000 × 2 × 2 cm, 2 Nos. both made from the procured 20 gauge GI sheet; Key 6 mm ϕ, 56 mm length), Cross connectors (6 mm ϕ rod -U clamp, 34 Nos.), Wooden end frames (5 × 5 cm wood, 0.15 m^3), nuts and bolts (6 mm ϕ, 35 mm long, 70 sets) and miscellaneous items like nails, hinges and latches as per requirement.

9.3.2 Preparation of Materials

Hoops are the integral part of the greenhouse frame. Hoops are formed in semicircular shape by bending the GI pipe. For bending, pipe bender is used, which can bend pipe in any desired radius. About 30 cm length on each end remains unbent which enables the ends to easily fit into the foundation pieces. Foundation pipes are meant to provide a firm support to the hoops and to secure the polygrip firmly. GI pipes of 25 mm (class A) and 85 cm length are used as foundation pieces. A 10 cm piece of MS flat is centrally welded to the one end of pipe and a hole of 8 mm is drilled at 10 cm distance from the other end. The flat welded end is put in a hole dug to a depth of 70 cm grouting with concrete. A 15 cm length of pipe remains above ground level to hold hoops and poly grip assembly.

The foundation pipes are spaced 1.25 m apart in parallel rows and it should be seen that the top of these pipes are at the same elevation. The end frame structures should have provision for a door and installation of environmental control equipment. For smaller greenhouse (up to 50 m^2) door is provided on one side while the medium and large greenhouses may have doors on both ends. The door frame (60 × 170 cm) is fabricated from 5 × 5 cm wood sections. The door is hinged and the open area is covered with either polyethylene film or any rigid plastic. For the lateral supports, rings of 3.5 cm ϕ are made at one end and a right angle hook on the other. During assembly the ring end encircles the foundation pipe which is put on before arranging the hoops. The other end of the lateral support is hooked to the end frame. Four lateral supports are provided at the four corners.

The function of polygrip assembly is to secure the polyethylene covering to the foundation pipes so that it can withstand the wind load and also avoiding the film puncture. The polygrip mechanism is made from 20 gauge GI sheet. Strips of 4 cm and 13 cm width with the available length are cut from the sheet. The 4 cm strip is bent centrally to form a right angle section. The 13 cm strip is bent in the shape of a channel with its edges rounded (Fig. 9.2). MS rod of 6 mm ϕ and 56 mm long pieces are used for positioning channel, angle and polyethylene film sandwiched in between and keeping these under pressure. The polyethylene film is stretched and these MS rod pieces are put at a distance of 50 cm, holding the right angle strip against the channel along the whole length of the greenhouse on both sides. The UV-stabilized LDPE film of 150 to 200 micron thickness and width of 7 m is recommended for greenhouse glazing. The film is secured to both sides along the length using the polygrip mechanism and to end frames with wood nails. The ridge line mechanism keeps the hoops at equidistance and increases the structural rigidity of the greenhouse structure by inter connecting the hoops. A 15 mm ϕ GI pipe fastened

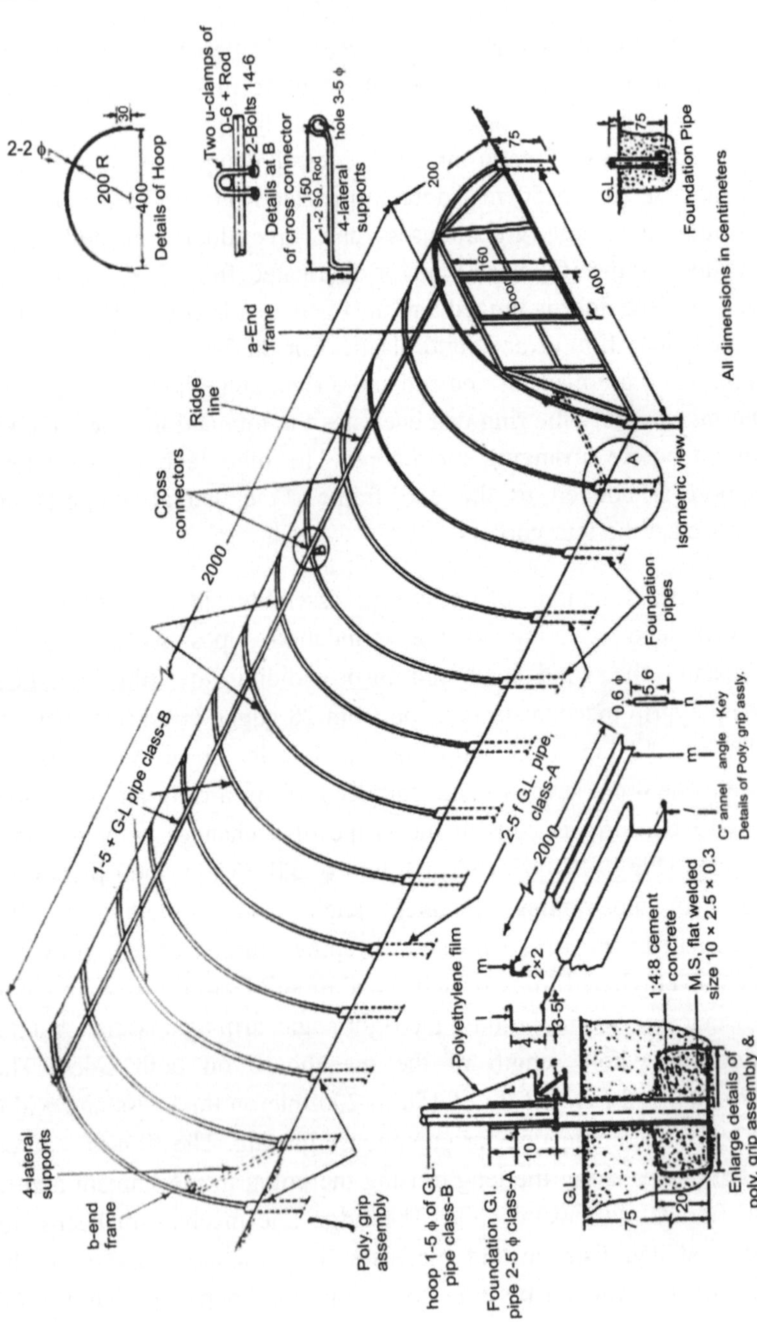

Fig. 9.2 Constructional details of pipe framed greenhouse.

at the ridge line maintains the hoops spacing and they are firmly secured to the hoops by the ridge line grip mechanism, which is fabricated from MS rods, looped over the crossing of the ridge and tightened with a bolt.

9.3.3 Procedure of Construction

A 4 m × 20 m rectangular area is marked on the site, preferably orienting the longer dimension in east-west direction. This rectangle will act as the floor plan of the greenhouse. Make sure that the adjacent sides are at right angles, which can be ensured by maintaining the two diagonals of the rectangle equal. Mark four points on the four comers of the rectangle. Start from one comer point and move along the length of the marked rectangle, marking a point every 1.25 m distance until reaching the other corner (16 bays, 17 points). The procedure is repeated on the other side of the rectangle.

Dig 10 cm ϕ holes to 70 cm depth on all marked points with the help of bucket auger or a crow bar. This way a total of 34 holes on both the parallel sides of the greenhouse floor are obtained. Splice poly grip sections of available lengths formed according to the drawing into two 20 m lengths. Fix the prefabricated polygrip channels to the foundation pipes on 1.25 m spacing with the help of 6 mm ϕ bolts. Set these assemblies on temporary supports between the holes with the foundation pipes hanging vertically in the holes and the tops straight and at constant elevation. Pour cement concrete mix of 1:3:6 around foundation pipes such that the lower 15 to 20 cm pipe ends are covered in concrete (Fig. 9.2). The concrete is compacted around the foundation pipes with the help of the crow bar and is allowed to cure for 2 to 3 days. After curing, fill the soil around the foundation pipes to the ground level and compact it well. Position end frames on the two ends. Mark the position of legs and dig holes for the fixing of legs. Now install both the end frames vertically and duly compact soil .on the legs. Put the ringside of lateral support members on adjacent foundation pipe to the corner, and other side is hooked to the end frame. Put all the hoops in the foundation pipes such that the straight portion of hoop is inserted into the foundation and rests on the bolt used for fixing of the polygrip channel. Make a 20 m long ridge pipe by splicing 15 mm pipes together. Put the 20 m long pipe at the ridge line of the hoops. Use cross connectors on the ridge line pipe such that one half of it remains on the one side of the hoop and the other half on the other side. Put two bolts of 6 mm in the holes provided in the ends of the cross connector. Tie a few of them with the help of nuts.

Repeat the procedure for joining all the hoops with ridge line pipe. While fixing cross connectors, the distance between the hoops or cross connectors should be maintained 1.25 m center to center. This grip mechanism will provide a firm grip of the ridge line pipe and hoops at right angles without allowing for slippage. Spread polyethylene film over the structure from one end to the other without wrinkles and keeping the edges together. Place polyethylene film between the polygrip channel and right angle strip and secure them under pressure with the help of the iron rods. The film is stretched gently and fixed on the other parallel side by poly grip. This way the polyethylene is secured on both the longer sides. On the other two remaining ends, polyethylene is nailed to the end frames using wooden battens and nails. The remaining portion of the end frames is covered with polyethylene film, which is secured with wooden battens and nails. If fiberglass or other transparent rigid material can be obtained, it can be used on the ends. Mechanical ventilation, heating and cooling equipment is installed on the frames as per the crop requirement.

REVIEW QUESTIONS

1. Supply and explain the floor plan of a typical greenhouse firm capable of future expansion.
2. Describe briefly the construction aspects of glass greenhouse.
3. Give the material requirement for the construction of 4 × 20 m pipe framed greenhouse.
4. Discuss the methods of preparation of different materials required for the pipe framed greenhouse construction.

5. Provide the step by step procedure of construction of pipe framed greenhouse.

6. Explain the functions of the following with suitable sketches:

   (a) Foundation pipes

   (b) Lateral supports

   (c) Polygrip mechanism

   (d) Ridge line mechanism

Chapter 10

CONSTRUCTION OF LOW COST WOODEN FRAMED PLASTIC FILM GREENHOUSE

Low cost greenhouse is a simple structure, constructed with locally available materials, such as bamboo and timber. The UV-stabilized LDPE film is used as cladding materials. Unlike conventional greenhouse, no specific control devices for regulating environmental factors inside the greenhouse are provided. However, simple techniques are adopted for manipulating temperature and relative humidity. Using shading materials and nets can reduce light intensity. The temperature can be reduced during warm season by opening all side walls. Such structure is used as rain shelter for raising crop. Otherwise, inside temperature is increased in the greenhouse when side walls are covered with plastic film. This chapter deals with the material requirement, material preparation and the detailed construction procedure of low cost wooden greenhouse.

10.1 Material Requirement

The materials required for the construction of low cost wooden greenhouse (Fig. 10.1) are: Wooden poles (a smaller 5 cm and larger

7 to 10 cm ϕ), GI wire (4 mm ϕ), MS strips, metallic hooks, wooden supports (5 cm ϕ, 15 cm length), UV-stabilized LDPE film, 1000 gauge black LDPE film, coal tar or bitumen or creosote, ordinary LDPE film roll and miscellaneous items like wooden pegs, ropes and nails.

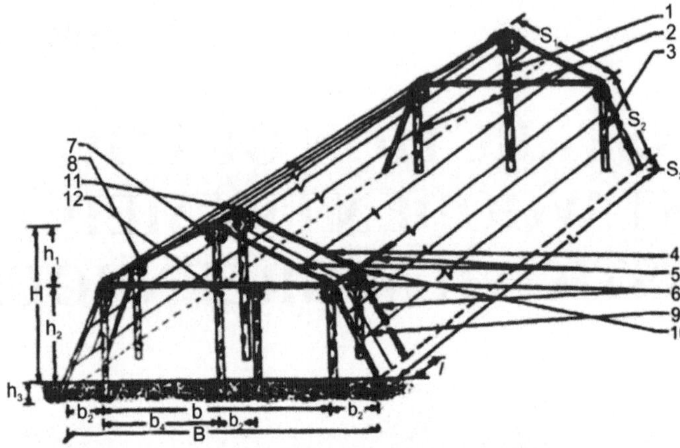

1,2,3 - large diameter (7 to 10) wooden pole
7,8 - small diameter wooden pole (L-15 m)
10,11 - MS strip
L - Length of the greenhouse
H - Middle height of greenhouse
b - Width of the greenhouse at the top
b_2 - Width of entrance gate
S_2 - Diagonal width at the side
4,5,6 - Small diameter (5 cm) wooden pole
9 - 4 mm GI wire
1_2 - Metallic hook (curtain supporter)
l - Bay distance (L = nxl) where n = No.of days
h_2 - Side height of greenhouse
b_1 - Extended width of the greenhouse
S_1 - Diagonal width at the top
S_3 - Side foundation depth

Fig. 10.1 Schematic diagram of low cost wooden greenhouse.

10.2 Preparation of Materials

The material required should be obtained and prepared according to the specifications (Fig. 10.2). Two sizes of wooden poles, for instance eucalyptus stems, are normally used. One is of larger diameter around 7 to 10 cm and other is smaller around 5 cm. The larger size stems are used for the main structure and the smaller size is utilized for the supporting structure. A proper selection of these poles will help in maintaining the symmetry of the structure. The length required for the poles are based on the dimensions of the different members in the structure and the quantity required. GI wire of 2 to 4 mm diameter is utilized to support the cladding material (UV-stabilized plastic film). A network of this wire is created after the completion of the total structure. The total length is calculated based on the requirement. The black plastic film in rolls of 7 to 10 cm widths could be prepared to wrap around the foundation poles. The weight of the film required is based on the dimension of the wrapping. A roll of 10 cm width LDPE film or left-over UV-stabilized LDPE film should be prepared to wrap all the poles, joints and wires to avoid direct contact with the UV-stabilized LDPE film. The 10 cm width film roll can be prepared from unutilized UV-stabilized LDPE film or simple LDPE roll by using a knife or scissors. Wooden pegs are required to mark the field.

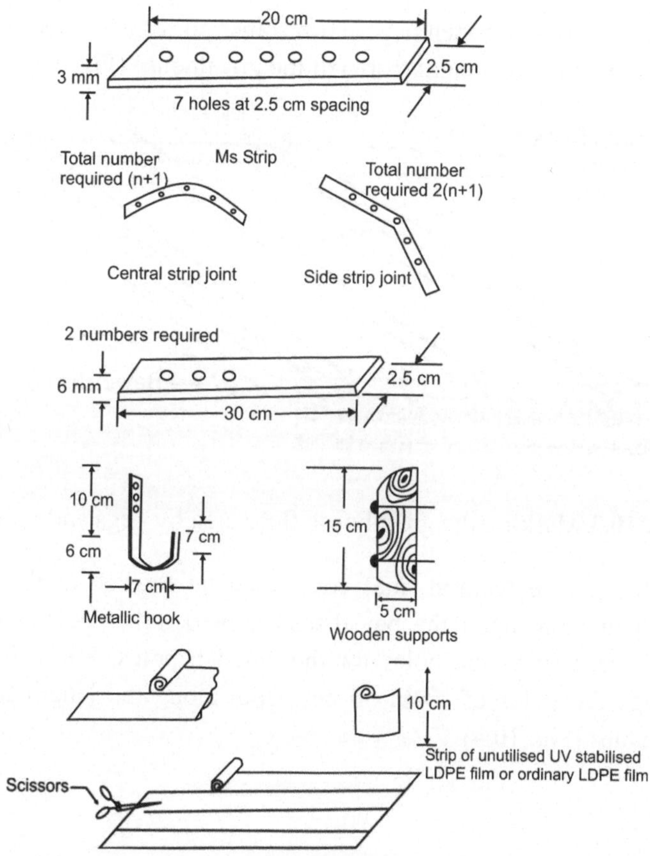

Fig. 10.2 Preparation of materials for low cost wooden greenhouse.

10.3 Construction Procedure

Site selection and orientation of the greenhouse plays a very important role in its efficiency. An ideal site should have proper drainage so that the surface water is drained away from the greenhouse. The east-west orientation of the length of the greenhouse maintains better light level in winter as compared to the north-south oriented one. However, the orientation has to be decided at specific site location depending on wind direction, available wind break, as well as movement of sunlight.

First determine the floor area (length × width) to be covered by the greenhouse. Mark the four comers on the ground based on the dimensions. Insert wooden pegs at the comer points and tie a rope all round to mark the rectangular area of the greenhouse (Fig. 10.3).

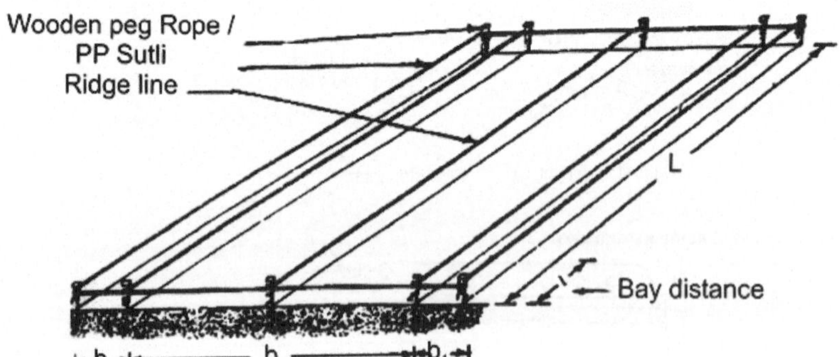

Fig. 10.3 Marking the greenhouse floor area by pegs and ropes.

Ridge line (central line) could also be marked at the same time. Depending upon the bay distance, mark other points on the ground for digging the holes for the wooden poles. Following the markings dig holes of about 50 cm depth along the length for the larger poles (Fig. 10.4).

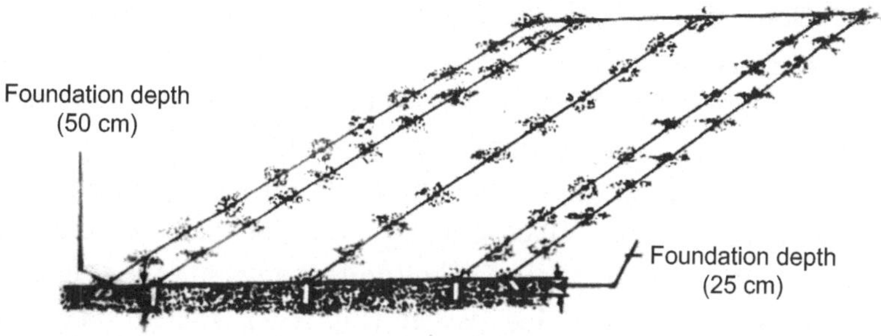

Fig. 10.4 Digging holes for posts on the marked locations.

Make ready all large diameter poles in their respective lengths and treat them for termite and moisture attack. This can be done by coating them with coal tar or bitumen and wrapping the poles with 1000 gauge black LDPE film with the help of polypropylene sutli. Creosote, a dark oily wood preservative distilled from coal tar, can also be used for protecting the stems from termite attack (Fig. 10.5).

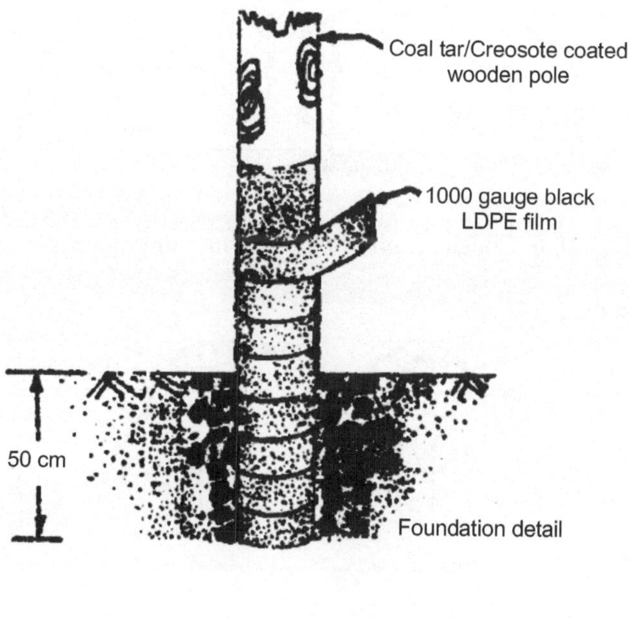

Fig. 10.5 Termite and moisture proofing of poles.

Hoist large poles in the length-wise direction and compact the foundation by using gravel and stones. Wooden supports, the blocks which support the poles at joints, should be prepared as described earlier and nail them to the larger poles for building up the structure. Complete one bay structure first and construct the subsequent bays one after another (Fig. 10.6), leaving space for the small diameter poles, which are used to join the bays afterwards. Put the side poles as per the marks identified earlier (Fig.10.4). Join all the bays together with the smaller diameter poles using MS strip. The MS strip should be nailed properly for firm grip and better strength (Fig. 10.7).

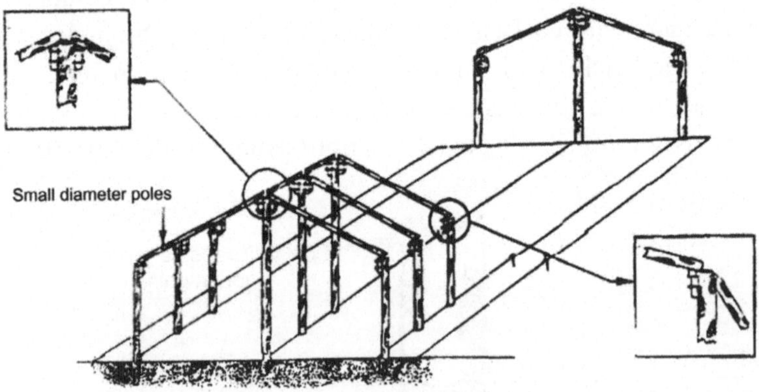

Fig. 10.6 Construction of bay structure in sequence.

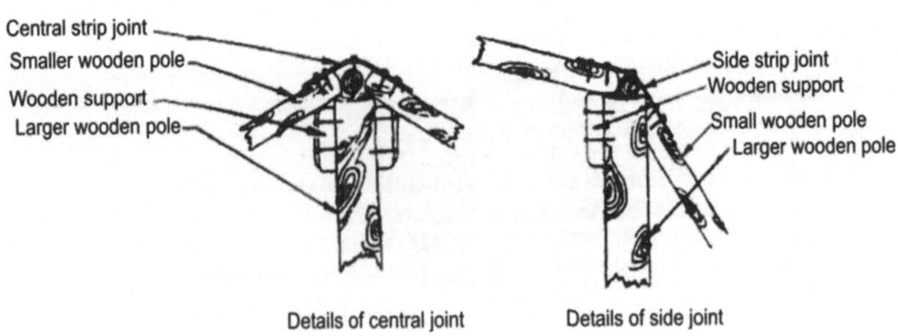

Fig. 10.7 Detail of central and side joints.

Now the structure is covered with a network of 4 mm GI wire to support the cladding material (Fig. 10.8). Wrap the LDPE film roll on all the poles which would come in contact with UV-stabilized LDPE film. This is done to check the exposure of any sharp points to the UV-stabilized LDPE film, which can thus be damaged and also to avoid degradation of the film due to migration of resins from the wooden poles.

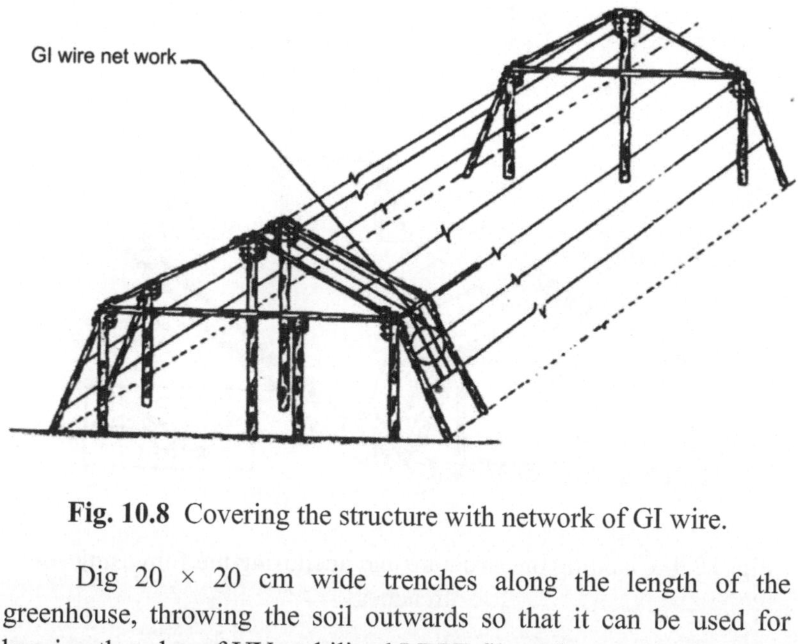

Fig. 10.8 Covering the structure with network of GI wire.

Dig 20 × 20 cm wide trenches along the length of the greenhouse, throwing the soil outwards so that it can be used for burying the edge of UV-stabilized LDPE film (Fig. 10.9). Make sure that the soil used for covering this film is free from rocks or any sharp objects. Cladding the structure was done using UV-stabilized LDPE film. Since UV-stabilized LDPE film is made of low-density polyethylene, sharp objects can damage the film rendering it useless. Proper care therefore, need be taken in rendering all the surfaces in contact with the film are smooth.

UV-stabilized LDPE film is generally available in the width of 7 m. It is clad across the length of the greenhouse. The joints between two lengths are heat sealed to avoid leakage or flapping due to wind action and to make the structure air tight. An overlap of 12 to

15 cm is kept for proper sealing. The length of UV-stabilized LDPE film is determined by measuring the total perimeter of the structure along its cross-section.

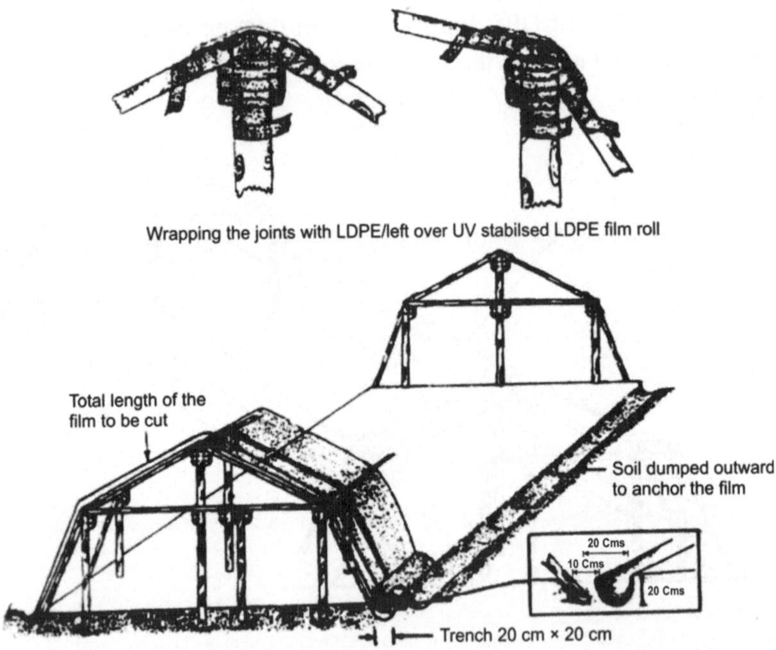

Fig. 10.9 Cladding the structure and anchoring the film using soil trenches.

Check for rough edges on the framework, which may tear or puncture the polyethylene film and wrap any such rough edges with strips of polyethylene. Rollout the polyethylene sheet along one side of structure, keeping one long edge to the top. Pull the leading edge over the frame, leaving a similar, surplus on each side. Fill one side of greenhouse trench anchoring the film with soil and pull the polyethylene film on other side of the greenhouse to maintain tension and bury the film firmly on the other side. The most vital element in the cladding operation is to make sure that the film is appropriately taut so that there is no sagging. This is preferably to be done in the sunlight. Care should be taken that the film lies flat against the two sides and along the bottom of the trench when it is buried. Cut away surplus film and cut out a rough entrance shape at ends, making sure to allow sufficient film overlap for fixing to door frames. Wrap films around end frames and nail it with wooden battens. The sides of the greenhouse are covered with a separate film. The roll-up door flaps can also be made from the film (Fig. 10.10). The bottom edge is secured by a smaller diameter wooden pole on which the flap can be rolled up to any height for ventilation and access. Hooks are nailed at the end spans to hold the rolled film. During daytime the door flap curtain should be rolled up from both sides to facilitate ventilation. Proper workmanship will help in developing a sturdy structure (Fig. 10.11) without damaging the UV-stabilized LDPE film.

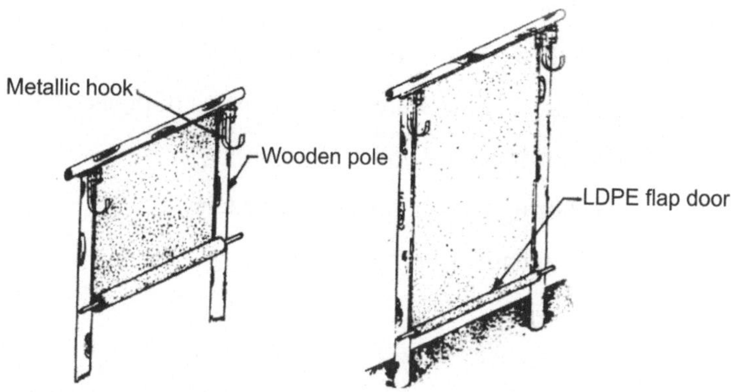

Fig. 10.10 Roll-up door flap arrangement for the greenhouse.

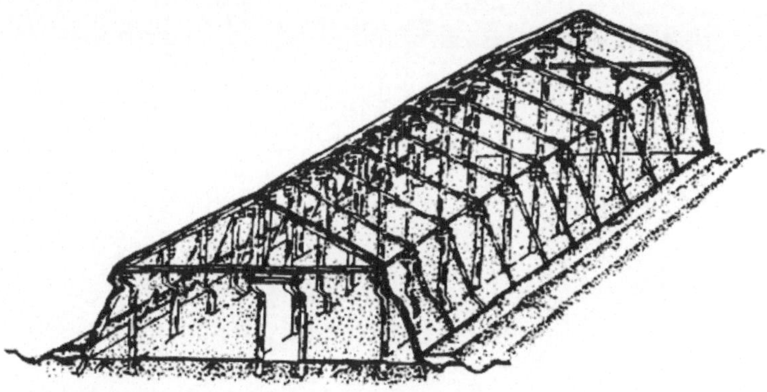

Fig. 10.11 Completed low cost wooden greenhouse structure.

This will increase the total life period of greenhouse structure as well as the longevity of the UV-stabilized LDPE film.

REVIEW QUESTIONS

1. Give the material requirement for a low cost wooden greenhouse.
2. Describe the preparation of materials for the construction of low cost wooden greenhouse.
3. Describe the step by step procedure of construction of low cost wooden greenhouse.
4. Supply the sketches for the following:
   (a) Termite and moisture attack proofing of poles
   (b) Details of central and side joints
   (c) Anchoring the film using soil trenches
   (d) Roll-up flap door arrangement

Chapter 11

GREENHOUSE COOLING

Ventilation and cooling of greenhouse environment are essential during summer and winter as well. While summer cooling is done using evaporative cooling systems, the winter cooling uses convection-tube with pressurizing fans and exhaust fans. Although the warming phenomenon due to greenhouse effect is desirable inside greenhouse, occasions arise to cool the greenhouse environment to guard the crops from the ill effects of overheating. Greenhouse cooling during summer and winter should be thought essentially of maintaining the desirable temperature and air quality by moving and mixing for efficient crop production. Greenhouse cooling requires that large volume of air to be brought into the greenhouse. Recommendations for standard flow rates of ventilation per square area of greenhouse are available. Correction factors from standard tables should be incorporated to the recommended standard air flow rate to account for site elevation, light intensity, temperature rise, distance between cooling pads and temperature difference between the inside and outside of the greenhouse. Selection of the fan, pad area, and convection-tube can also be obtained from the standard tables after calculation of air requirement. This chapter deals with estimation of air exchange rates in active summer and winter cooling designs along with numerical examples.

11.1 Design of Active Summer Cooling System

The rate of air exchange is measured in cubic meters per minute (cmm). The National Greenhouse Manufacturers Association (NGMA) indicates in its 2004 standards and guidelines for ventilating and cooling greenhouses that a rate of removal of 2.5 cmm/m^2 of greenhouse floor is sufficient. This applies to a greenhouse under 305 m in elevation, with an interior light intensity not exceeding 53.8 klux and an air temperature rise of 4°C from pad to fans. Standard tables of correction factors of the rate of air removal are available to account for any deviation from these standard conditions. Since it is relatively tedious to calculate the air volume using this method, a direct value of 3.4 to 5.2 cmm/m^2 of floor area recommended by Willits (1993) can be used.

The rate of air removal from the greenhouse must increase as the elevation of the greenhouse site increases. The density of air decreases and becomes lighter with increase in elevation. The ability of air to remove solar heat from the greenhouse depends upon its weight and not its volume. Thus, a larger volume of air must be drawn through the greenhouse at high elevations than that is drawn through at low elevations in order to have an equivalent cooling effect. Hence, the values of elevation factor (F_{elev}) are directly proportional to the elevation. The values of elevation factors, used to correct the rate of air removal for a particular elevation are listed in Table 11.1.

Table 11.1 Correction Factors of the Rate of Air Removal for Elevation Above Sea Level.

Elevation above sea level (m)	**<300**	**300**	**600**	**900**	**1200**	**1500**	**1800**	**2100**	**2400**
F_{elev}	1.00	1.04	1.08	1.12	1.16	1.20	1.25	1.30	1.36

Source: National Greenhouse Manufacturers Association (2004)

The rate of air removal is also depends upon the light intensity in the greenhouse. As light intensity increases, the heat input from the sun increases, requiring a greater rate of air removal from the greenhouse. Hence, the values of light factor (F_{light}) vary directly with the light intensity. The values of light factors used to adjust the rate of air removal are listed in Table 11.2. In general, an intensity of 53.8 klux is accepted as a desirable level for crops. Any excess light intensity can also be controlled either with a coat of shading compound on the greenhouse covering or with a screen material above the plants in the greenhouse.

Table 11.2 Correction Factors of the Rate of Air Removal for Maximum Light Intensity in the Greenhouse.

Light intensity (klux)	**43.1**	**48.4**	**53.8**	**59.2**	**64.6**	**70.0**	**75.3**	**80.1**	**86.1**
F_{light}	0.80	0.90	1.00	1.10	1.20	1.30	1.40	1.50	1.60

Source : National Greenhouse Manufacturers Association (2004)

Solar energy warms the air as it passes from the pad to the exhaust fans. Usually, a 4°C rise in temperature is tolerated across the greenhouse. If it becomes important to have uniform temperature across the greenhouse, it will be necessary to raise the velocity of the air movement through the greenhouse. To maintain less temperature difference across the greenhouse more air is to be circulated. Hence, the temperature factor (F_{temp}) increases as the difference in temperature across pad to fan decreases. The temperature factors used for various possible temperature rises are given in Table 11.3.

Table 11.3 Correction Factors of the Rate of Air Removal for a given Pad-to-fan Temperature Rises.

Temperature rise (°C)	**5.6**	**5.0**	**4.4**	**3.9**	**3.3**	**2.8**	**2.2**
F_{temp}	0.70	0.78	0.88	1.00	1.17	1.40	1.75

Source: National Greenhouse Manufacturers Association (2004)

The pad and fans should be placed on opposite walls, either end walls or side walls of the greenhouse (Fig. 11.1) and the distance between them is important. A distance of 30 to 61 m is the best. The size of the exhaust fan should be selected to achieve proper temperature difference and good circulation. If the pad to fan distance is less, then there is less opportunity time for the flowing air to cool the surroundings; whereas with very large distance uniform cooling is not possible as fans may not pull enough air through the pads. To achieve a given degree of cooling, more amount of air is required when pad to fan distance is less and vice versa. So the velocity of incoming air is to be modified accordingly. The velocity factors (F_{vel}) used to compensate for pad to fan distance are listed in Table 11.4.

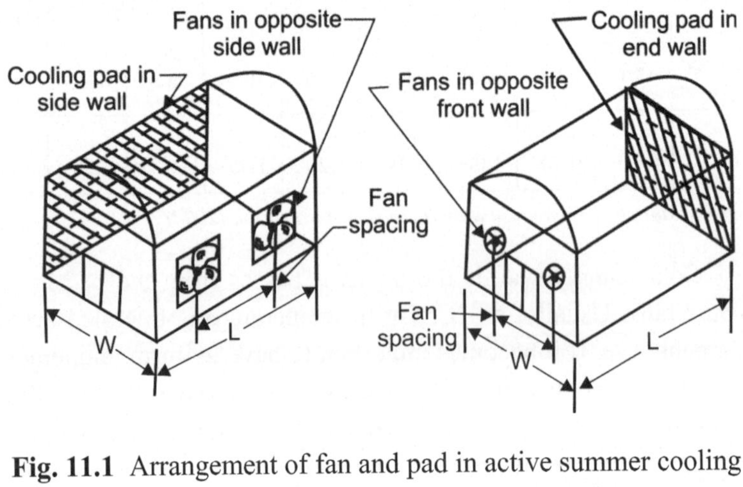

Fig. 11.1 Arrangement of fan and pad in active summer cooling system.

The rate of air removal required for a specific greenhouse can be calculated using the factors given in Table 11.1 through 11.4. Firstly, the rate of air removal required for a greenhouse is determined under standard conditions (Q_{std}) using the following equation:

$$Q_{std} = L \times W \times 2.5$$

where, L is the length and W is the width of greenhouse.

Table 11.4 Correction Factors of the Rate of Air Removal for a given. Pad-to-Fan Distances.

Pad-to-fan distance (m)	**6.1**	**7.6**	**9.1**	**10.7**	**12.2**	**13.7**	**15.2**	**16.8**	**18.3**
F_{vel}	2.24	2.00	1.83	1.69	1.58	1.48	1.41	1.35	1.29
Pad-to-fan distance (m)	**19.8**	**21.3**	**22.9**	**24.4**	**25.9**	**27.4**	**29.0**	**>30.5**	
F_{vel}	1.24	1.20	1.16	1.12	1.08	1.05	1.02	1.00	

Source: National Greenhouse Manufacturers Association (2004)

Now, the standard rate of air removal is adjusted by multiplying it by the larger of the following two factors: F_{house}, or F_{vel}. The value of F_{vel} is read directly from Table 11.4, whereas F_{house} is calculated from the following equation:

$$F_{house} = F_{elev} \times F_{light} \times F_{temp}$$

Thus, the final adjusted (Q_{adj}) capacity of the exhaust fans must be:

$$Q_{adj} = Q_{std} \times (F_{house} \text{ or } F_{vel})$$

The size and number of exhaust fans must be selected next. The collective capacity of the fans should be at least equal to the rate of air removal required at a static water pressure of 30 Pa. If slant wall housing fans are used, which has the fan outside the louvers, the fans should be rated at 15 Pa static water pressure. The static pressure value takes into account the resistance the fans meet in drawing air through the pad and the fan itself. Air-delivery ratings for various sizes of fans are listed in Table 11.5. Fans should not be spaced more than 7.6 m apart. The required capacity of each fan in this case can be determined by dividing the Q_{adj} by the number of fans required. These fans are selected for their rated performance levels from the tables and are evenly spaced in the greenhouse, at plant height if possible, to guarantee a uniform flow of air through the plants. The excelsior (wood fiber) pads of 2.5 to 4 cm thick are generally used. These are replaced annually and they support an airflow rate of 45 cmm/m^2. Cross-fluted cellulose pads come in units of 30 cm wide and are 5, 10, 15 or 30 cm thick. They can last up to 10 years, and the commonly used 10 cm thick pad can accommodate an air intake of 75 cmm/m^2. An arrangement of excelsior pad on the end wall and cross fluted cellulose cooling pad on the side is shown in Figs. 11.2 and 11.3, respectively.

Fig. 11.2 Excelsior cooling pad on the end wall of greenhouse.

Fig. 11.3 Cross-fluted cellulose cooling pad on the side wall of greenhouse.

The total area of pad required is determined by dividing the volume of air that must be removed from the greenhouse in unit time by the volume of air that can be moved through a square meter of pad or can directly be obtained from Table 11.5.

Table 11.5 Correction Factors of the Rate of Air Removal for a given Pad-to-Fan distances.

Fan size (cm)	Horse power (hp)	Rate at 30 Ps static pressure (cmm)	Pad area per fan (m^2)		
			Excelsior	10 cm Cellulose	15 cm Cellulose
61	0.25	127	2.8	4.5	1.2
	0.33	161	3.5	2.1	1.5
	0.50	184	4.0	2.4	1.8
	0.75	215	4.7	2.8	2.0
76	0.33	209	4.6	2.8	2.0
	0.50	249	5.5	3.3	2.3
	0.75	289	6.3	3.8	2.7
91	0.33	249	5.5	3.3	2.3
	0.50	300	6.6	4.0	2.9
	0.75	359	7.9	4.7	3.4
	1.00	402	8.8	5.3	3.8
107	0.50	354	7.8	4.6	3.3
	0.75	425	9.3	5.6	4.0
	1.00	475	10.4	6.3	4.5
122	0.50	416	9.1	5.5	3.9
	0.75	504	11.1	6.7	4.7
	1.00	555	12.2	7.2	5.2
137	1.00	648	14.2	8.5	6.1
	1.50	730	16.0	9.7	6.9

Source: Acme Engineering and Manufacturing Corporation, Muskogee, OK (1993)

Water must be delivered to the top of a 10 cm thick cross-fluted cellulose pad at the rate of 6.2 l/min/m of pad, with proper distribution pipes and holes arrangement. The flow rate for a 15 cm pad is 9.3 l/min/m of pad. The sump volume should be 30.5 l/m^2 for

10 cm thick pad, and 40.7 l/m^2 for 15 cm thick pad. These sump volumes are designed for an operating water level at half the depth of the tank and will provide space to accommodate water returning from the pad when the system is turned off. Water should be delivered to the top of an excelsior pad at the rate of 13.6 l/min/m of pad, regardless of the height of the pad. Since all water will return to the sump when the system is turned off, a sump capacity of 19 l/m of pad is required.

NUMERICAL EXAMPLE

Design a summer evaporative cooling system with the following requirements. Consider a single greenhouse 15 m wide and 30 m long located at an elevation of 915 m. The greenhouse has a moderate coat of shading compound on it, providing the maximum light intensity of 53.8 klux. A 4°C rise in temperature can be tolerated from pad to fans. Use a 10 cm thick cross-fluted cellulose cooling system for the greenhouse. (Nelson, 2003)

Solution:

The step by step calculations involved in the design are as follows:

1. Multiply the greenhouse floor width by the length and by the recommended 2.5 cmm/m^2 to determine the quantity of air to be removed per minute under standard conditions

$$Q_{std} = L \times W \times 2.5 = 15 \text{ m} \times 30 \text{ m} \times 2.5 \text{ cmm/m}^2$$

$$= 1125 \text{ cmm}$$

2. Determine the factor for the house as described earlier, using Tables 11.1 through 11.3

$$F_{house} = F_{elev} \times F_{light} \times F_{temp}$$

$$= 1.12 \times 1.0 \times 1.0 = 1.12$$

3. Look up the factor for velocity in Table 11.4. Select two opposite walls that are 30 to 61 m apart or as close to 30 m apart as possible, for installation of the pad and fans. The end walls, which are 30 m apart, should be used in this case

$$F_{vel} = 1.00$$

4. Multiply the Q_{std} value by either F_{house} or F_{vel}, whichever factor is larger. This is the adjusted volume of air to be expelled from the greenhouse each minute

$$Q_{adj} = Q_{std} \times F_{house} = 1125 \text{ cmm} \times 1.12 = 1260 \text{ cmm}$$

5. Determine the number of fans needed. Since they should not be over 7.6 m apart, divide the length of the wall housing the fans by 7.6 m

$$15 \text{ m} / 7.6 \text{ m} = 2 \text{ fans}$$

6. Determine the size of the fans needed by dividing the Q_{adj} of air to be removed by the number of fans needed

$$Q_{adj}/2 = 1260 \text{ cmm} / 2 = 630 \text{ cmm per fan}$$

7. Select two fans of the size determined earlier and space them at equidistance on one end of the greenhouse. The required fans can be selected from the manufacturer equipment list (Table 11.5). From the table, 2 Nos. of 137 cm fans with 1 hp motors would be selected.

8. The pad area is determined from the recommendation. One square meter is required for each 75 cmm of fan capacity.

$$\text{Pad area} = (\text{Fan capacity} / 75) \times \text{Number of fans}$$

$$= (630 \text{ cmm} / 75 \text{ cmm/m}^2) \times 2 = 16.8 \text{ m}^2$$

Approximately the same value could be read directly from Table 11.5 (8.5 m^2 per fan).

9. The pad must cover the width of the wall in which it is to be installed (15 m in this example). The height of the pad is determined by dividing the total pad area by its width.

$$\text{Pad height} = \text{Pad area} / \text{Pad width}$$

$$= 16.8 \text{ m}^2 / 15 \text{ m} = 1.1 \text{ m}$$

A 1.22 m tall pad should be purchased. Hence,

$$\text{Actual pad area} = 15 \text{ m} \times 1.22 \text{ m} = 18.3 \text{ m}^2.$$

10. The pump capacity is based on a standard flow rate of 6.2 lpm/m for 10 cm pad multiplied by the length of the pad. The pump should be selected to have this flow rate for the given head under which it must operate. The head is the

distance from the water surface in the sump to the top of the pads

Pump capacity = 6.2 1pm/m × 15 m = 93 lpm

11. The sump size at a standard volume rate of 30.5 1/ m^2 for 4 inch pad. Therefore to a pad area of 18.3 m^2

Sump volume = 30.5 1/ m^2 × 18.3 m^2 = 558 1

11.2 Design of Active Winter Cooling System

During winter, the outside air temperature will be less than that is inside the greenhouse. Therefore simple mixing of the outside ambient air by convection tubes does the actual winter cooling. In active winter cooling systems, under standard conditions a volume of 0.61 cmm of air should be removed from the greenhouse for each square meter of floor area. The air volume obtained by multiplying the floor area by this value would define the capacity of the exhaust fan.. If a lower inside temperature is desired, cold air must be introduced into the greenhouse at a greater rate. Hence, in active winter cooling, the winter factor (F_{winter}) based on temperature difference between inside and outside air vary inversely with the required temperature difference. The compensating factors to be used in active winter cooling are given in Table 11.6.

Table 11.6 Correction Factors of Standard Rate of Air Removal in a Winter Greenhouse Cooling System based on Temperature Difference.

Temperature Difference (°C)	**10.0**	**9.4**	**8.9**	**8.3**	**7.8**	**7.2**	**6.7**	**6.1**	**5.6**	**5.0**
F_{winter}	0.83	0.88	0.94	1.00	1.07	1.15	1.25	1.37	1.50	16.7

Source: National Greenhouse Manufacturers Association (2004)

As in the case of summer cooling systems, standard conditions also specify an elevation under 305 m and a maximum interior light intensity of 53.8 klux. If other elevation or light intensity specifications are desired, factors must be selected from Tables 11.1

and 11.2 are used to correct the rate of air entry. Convection tubes are conventionally oriented from end to end in the greenhouse (Fig. 4.3). One convection tube placed down the center of the house will cool houses up to 9.1 m in width. Greenhouses 9.1 to 18.3 m wide are cooled by two tubes placed equidistant from the side walls across the greenhouse. Holes along the tube exist in pairs on the opposite vertical sides. The holes vary in size according to the volume of greenhouse to be cooled. The number and diameter of tubes needed to cool a greenhouse can be determined from Table 11.7. If two or more tubes are needed, they should be of equal size and should be spaced evenly across the greenhouse. Recommendations in Table 11.7 are based on an air flow rate approximately 518 cmm/m^2 of cross sectional area in the tube. When the greenhouse is large and the required number of 76 cm diameter tubes becomes cumbersome, tubes may be installed with air inlets in both ends. These inlets double the amount of cool air that can be brought in through a single tube.

Table 11.7 Air Distribution Tubes Required for Winter Cooling of Greenhouse of Various Sizes.

Greenhouse width	**Number (N) and Diameter (D in cm) of air distribution tubes for different greenhouse lengths**									
	15 m		**30 m**		**46 m**		**61 m**		**76 m**	
(m)	**N**	**D**	**N**	**D**	**N**	**D**	**N**	**D**	**N**	**D**
4.6	1	46	1	46	1	61	1	76	1	76
6.1	1	46	1	61	1	76	1	76	2	61
7.6	1	46	1	61	1	76	2	61	2	76
9.1	2	46	2	46	2	61	2	76	2	76
10.7	2	46	2	61	2	76	2	76	3	76
12.2	2	46	2	61	2	76	2	76	3	76
15.2	2	46	2	61	2	76	3	76	3	76

Source National Greenhouse Manufacturers Association (2004)

Note: Tubes run the length of the greenhouse and are spaced equidistantly across the greenhouse. Tubes derive cold air from a louvered air inlet on one side only.

NUMERICAL EXAMPLE

Design a winter convection tube cooling system for the following requirements. Consider a single greenhouse 15m wide and 30 m long located at an elevation of 915 m. The greenhouse has a moderate coat of shading compound on it, providing the maximum light intensity of 53.8 klux, and the desired interior-to-exterior temperature difference of 8°C. (Nelson, 2003)

Solution :

The step by step calculations involved in the design are as follows:

1. The capacity of the exhaust fan is equal to 0.61 cmm/m^2 times the greenhouse floor area under standard conditions.

$$Q_{std} = 0.61 \times 30 \times 15 = 275 \text{ cmm}$$

2. Correct the exhaust fan capacity for the deviations from standard conditions using interior-to-exterior temperature difference, elevation and light intensity from the standard tables.

$$Q_{adj} = Q_{std} \times F_{winter} \times F_{light}$$
$$= 275 \times 1.0 \times 1.12 \times 1.0 = 308 \text{ cmm}$$

Hence, an exhaust fan with a capacity of 308 cmm at a static water pressure of 30 Pa is needed.

3. The number of air distribution tubes can be determined from Table 11.7. Two 61 cm tubes are needed for this greenhouse having 15 m width and 30 m length.

4. The diameter of the individual holes along the side of distribution tubes and the distance between them must be decided next. The suppliers may specify the type of tubes. In general, the total area of all holes in a single tube should be 1.5 to 2 times the cross sectional area of the tube. The cross sectional area of 61 cm diameter ($\pi \times 61^2/4$) is 2922 cm^2; thus the combined area of all holes in a tube should be between 4,384 and 5.845 cm^2. As the required tube length increases, the distance between holes should increase to maintain a reasonable diameter hole. A hole spacing of 61 to 122 cm is

common. Once the holes spacing is decided, the hole diameter can be worked out after finding the number of holes the length of tube can accommodate as follows. From the above data, by considering the combined area of holes as 5845 cm^2, length of tube as 30 m (3000 cm) and hole spacing as 61 cm.

Number of holes per side of the tube = Length of tube / Hole spacing

$$= 3000 \text{ cm} / 61 \text{ cm} = 49$$

Number of holes in one tube = 2 × 49 = 98 [Since the holes are to be provide on both sides of the tube]

Area of the hole = Cross sectional area of tube / Number of holes

$$= 5845 \text{ cm}^2 / 98 = 59.64 \text{ cm}^2$$

Diameter of the hole = $(4 \times \text{Area of the hole}/\pi)^{1/2}$

$$= (4 \times 59.64 \text{ cm}^2 / \pi)^{1/2} = 8.71 \text{ cm}$$

Similarly, for the hole spacing of 122 cm, the number of holes/tube is 50, and the diameter of the holes is 12.2 cm. Calculations can also be carried out for the other combined area of the holes with different hole spacing.

5. The pressurizing fan in the inlet end of the convection tube should be equal to the exhaust fan in capacity. If this is not possible, then the pressurizing fan should be larger. The two pressurizing fans needed in this case should have a combined capacity of 308 cmm, which is equal to the exhaust fan capacity. Each pressurizing fan thus has half the capacity or 154 cmm at a static water pressure of 30 Pa.

REVIEW QUESTIONS

1. Differentiate between active summer and active winter cooling systems.
2. Describe briefly with suitable sketches the active summer cooling system and active winter cooling systems.

3. Why correction factors of rate of air removal are used with elevation, light intensity, pad-to-fan temperature rise, and pad-to-fan distance in active summer, and temperature difference in active winter cooling system and explain their physical significance?

4. Design a summer evaporative cooling system for the following requirements. Greenhouse is 20 m wide and 40 m long located at an elevation 600 m, experiencing a maximum light intensity of 70.0 klux, and a tolerable temperature difference from pad-to-fan is 5°C. A cross-fluted cellulose of 15 cm thick cooling system was used.
[Answer: Q_{std} = 2000 cmm; F_{house} = 1.09; F_{vel} = 1.00; Q_{adj} =2190 cmm; Three numbers of 54" fans of 1.5 hp each; Actual pad area = 30 m^2; Pump capacity = 186 lpm; Sump volume = 1190 l]

5. Design a winter convection tube cooling system for the following requirements. Size of the greenhouse is 20 m width and 40 m length located at an elevation 600 m, experiencing a maximum light intensity of 70.0 klux, and the desired interior-to exterior temperature difference is 7°C.
[Answer: Q_{std} = 488 cmm; Q_{adj} = 730 cmm; Two numbers of 76 cm diameter tubes are required; Number of holes at 61cm spacing = 130 with 9.5 cm diameter; Number of holes at 90 cm spacing = 90 with 11.2 cm diameter; Pressurizing fans combined capacity = 730 cmm with each fan having 365 cmm or larger]

Chapter 12

GREENHOUSE HEATING

The northern parts of India experience cold winters, where heating system need to be employed in the greenhouses along with cooling systems for hot summers. Whereas in southern parts of India, greenhouses need only cooling systems since the winter cold effect is not that severe. Greenhouse heating is required in cold weather conditions, wherein the entrapped heat is not sufficient for plant growth during the nights. The heat is always lost from the greenhouse when the surroundings are relatively cooler than the greenhouse environment. Heat must be supplied to a greenhouse at the same rate with which it is lost in order to maintain a desired temperature. Heat losses can occur in three different modes of heat transfer, namely conduction, convection, and radiation. Maintenance of desired higher temperature, compared with the surroundings, needs heating systems and heat distribution systems. For the purpose of greenhouse heating, apart from conventional systems, solar energy can also be used and the heat can be stored using water or rock storage. Different heat conservation practices are available to effectively utilize the heat energy. Heat requirement for A-frame and quonset greenhouse can be calculated using standard recommendations, geometry of structure, and simplified overall heat transfer equation. A brief discussion of the above aspects along with heat requirement calculation is covered in this chapter.

12.1 Modes of Heat Loss

The heating systems, in a continuous process, should supply the heat just enough to compensate which is lost. Most heat is lost by conduction through the covering materials of the greenhouse. Different materials, such as aluminum sash bars, glass, polyethylene, and cement partition walls, vary in conduction according to the rate at which each conducts heat from the warm interior to the colder exterior. A good conductor of heat looses more heat in a shorter time than a bad conductor and vice versa. There are only limited ways of insulating the covering material without blocking the light transmission. A dead air space between two coverings appears to be the best system. A saving of 40% of the heat requirement can be achieved when a second covering is applied. For example, a greenhouse covered with one layer of polyethylene loses 6.8 W of heat through each square meter of covering every hour when the outside temperature is 1°C lower than the inside. When second layer of polyethylene is added, only 3.97 W/m^2 is lost (40% reduction).

A second mode of heat loss is that of convection (air infiltration). Spaces between panes of glass or FRP and ventilators and doors permit the passage of warm air outward and cold air inward. A general assumption holds that the volume of air held in a greenhouse can be lost as often as once every 60 minutes in a double layer film plastic or polycarbonate panel greenhouse; every 40 minutes in a FRP or a new glass greenhouse; every 30 minutes in an old well maintained glass greenhouse; and every 15 minutes in an old poorly maintained glass greenhouse. About 10% of total heat loss from a structurally tight glass greenhouse occurs through infiltration loss.

A third mode of heat loss from a greenhouse is that of radiation. Warm objects emit radiant energy, which passes through air to colder objects without warming the air significantly. The colder objects become warmer. Glass, vinyl plastic, FRP, and water are relatively opaque to radiant energy, whereas polyethylene is not. Polyethylene greenhouses can lose considerable amounts of heat through radiation to colder objects outside, unless a film of moisture forms on the polyethylene to provide a barrier.

12.2 Heating Systems

The heating system must provide heat to the greenhouse at the same rate at which it is lost by conduction, infiltration, and radiation. There are three popular types of heating systems for greenhouses, namely unit heater, central heating system and radiation heating. The most common and least expensive is the unit heater system. In this system, warm air is blown from unit heaters that have self contained fireboxes. These heaters consist of three functional parts, namely, firebox, metal tube heat exchanger, and heat distribution fan. Fuel is combusted in a firebox to provide heat. The heat is initially contained in the exhaust, which rises through the inside of a set of thin walled metal tubes on its way to the exhaust stack. The warm exhaust transfers heat to the cooler metal walls of the tubes. Much of the heat is removed from the exhaust by the time it reaches the stack through which it leaves the greenhouse. A fan in the back of the unit heater draws in greenhouse air, passing it over the exterior side of the tubes and then out the front of the heater to the greenhouse environment again. The cool air passing over hot metal tubes is warmed and the air is circulated.

A second type of system is central heating system, which consists of a central boiler that produces steam or hot water, plus a radiating mechanism in the greenhouse to dissipate the heat. A central heating system can be more efficient than unit heaters, especially in large greenhouse ranges. In this system, two or more large boilers are in a single location. Heat is transported in the form of hot water or steam through pipe mains to the growing area, and several arrangements of heating pipes in greenhouse are possible (Fig. 12.1). The heat is exchanged from the hot water in a pipe coil on the perimeter walls plus an overhead pipe coil located across the greenhouse or an in-bed pipe coil located in the plant zone. Some greenhouses have a third pipe coil embedded in a concrete floor.

A set of unit heaters can be used in the place of the overhead pipe coil, obtaining heat from hot water or steam from the central boiler.

The third type of system is radiation heating system. In this system, gas is burned within pipes suspended overhead in the greenhouse. The warm pipes radiate heat to the plants. Low intensity infrared radiant heaters can save 30% or more of fuel compared to conventional heaters. Several of these heaters are installed in tandem in the greenhouse. Lower air temperatures are possible since only the plants and root substrate are heated directly by this mode of heating.

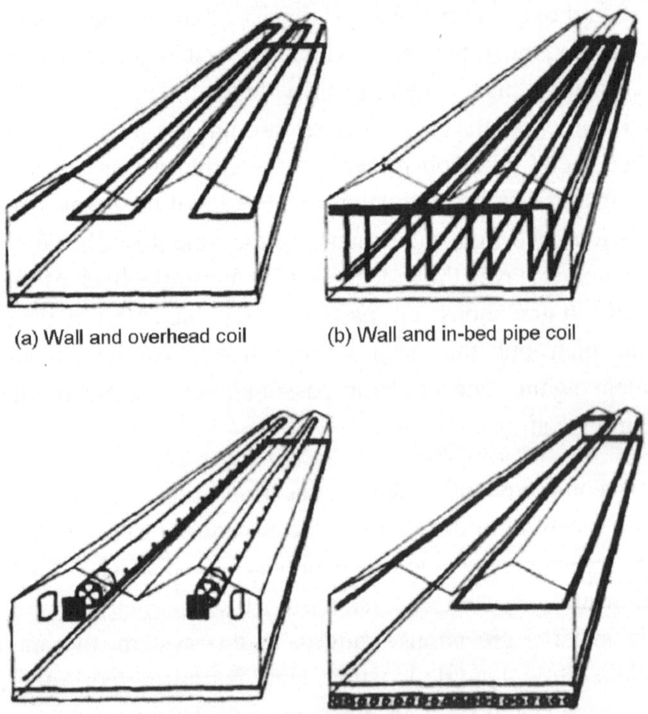

(a) Wall and overhead coil

(b) Wall and in-bed pipe coil

(c) Wall and overhead unit heaters

(d) Wall with limited overhead and in-floor coil

Fig. 12.1 Arrangement of heating pipe coils using steam or hot water in greenhouse.

The fourth possible type of system is the solar heating system, but it is still too expensive to be a viable option. Solar heating systems are found in hobby greenhouses and small commercial firms. Both water and rock energy storage systems are used in combination with solar energy. The high cost of solar heating systems discourages any significant use by the greenhouse industries.

12.3 Heat Distribution Systems

Heat is distributed from the unit heaters by one of two common methods. In the convection tube method, similar to winter cooling systems, warm air from unit heaters is distributed through a transparent polyethylene tube running through the length of the greenhouse. Heat escapes from the tube through holes on either side of the tube in small jet streams, which rapidly mix with the surrounding air and set up a circulation pattern to minimize temperature gradients.

The second method of heat distribution is horizontal airflow. In this system, the greenhouse may be visualized as a large box containing air, and it uses small horizontal fans for moving the air mass. The fans are located above plant height and are spaced about 15 m apart in two rows. Their arrangement is such that the heat originating at one corner of the greenhouse is directed from one side of the greenhouse to the opposite end and then back along the other side of the greenhouse. Proper arrangement of fans is necessary for effective distribution in horizontal airflow system for various greenhouse sizes. Both of these distribution systems can also be used for general circulation of air and for introducing cold outside air during winter cooling.

12.4 Solar Heating System

Solar heating is often used as a partial or total alternative to fossil fuel heating systems. Few solar heating systems exist in greenhouses today. The general components of solar heating system (Fig. 12.2) are collector, heat storage facility, exchanger to transfer the solar derived heat to the greenhouse air, backup heater to take over when solar heating does not suffice, and set of controls.

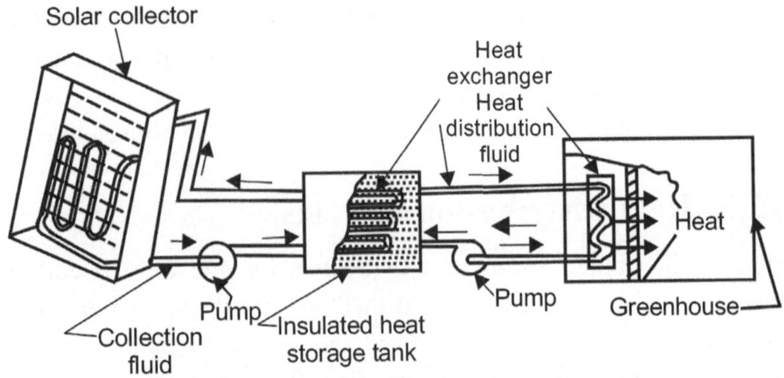

Fig. 12.2 A typical solar heating system for greenhouse.

Various solar heat collectors are in existence, but the type that has received greatest attention is the flat-plate collector. This consists of a flat black plate (rigid plastic, film plastic, sheet metal, or board) for absorbing solar energy. The plate is covered on the sun side by two or more transparent glass or plastic layers and on the backside by insulation. The enclosing layers serve to hold the collected heat within the collector. Water or air is passed through or over the black plate to absorb the entrapped heat and carry it to the storage facility. A greenhouse itself can be considered as a solar collector. Some of its collected heat is stored in the soil, plants, greenhouse frame, floor, and so on. The remaining excessive heat not required for plant growth is therefore vented to the outside. The excess vented heat could just as well be directed to a rock bed for storage and subsequent use during a period of heating. Collection of heat by flat-plate collectors is most efficient when the collector is positioned perpendicular to the sun rays at solar noon. Based on the locations, the heat derived can provide 20 to 50% of the heat requirement.

12.5 Water and Rock Storage

Water and rocks are the two most common materials for the storage of heat in the greenhouse. One kg of water can hold 4.23 kJ of heat for each 1°C rise in temperature. Rocks can store about 0.83 kJ for each 1°C. To store equivalent amounts of heat, a rock bed would have to be three times as large as a water tank. A water storage system is well adapted to a water collector and a greenhouse heating system which consists of a pipe coil or a unit heater with water coil. Heated water from the collector is pumped to the storage tank during the day. As and when heat is required, warm water is pumped from the storage tank to a hot water or steam boiler or into the hot water coil within a unit heater. Although the solar heated water will be cooler than the thermostat setting on the boiler, heat can be saved since the temperature of this water need be raised to reach the output temperature of water or steam from the boiler will be less. A temperature rise of 17°C above the ambient condition is expected during the daytime in solar storage units. Each kilogram of water can supply 71.1 kJ of heat, and each kilogram of rock 14.2 kJ, as it cools by 17°C.

A rock storage bed can be aptly used with an air-collector and forced air heating system. In this case, heated air from the collector, along with air excessively heated inside the greenhouse during the day, is forced through a bed of rocks (Fig. 12.3). The rocks absorb much of the heat. The rock bed may be located beneath the floor of the greenhouse or outside the greenhouse, and it should be well insulated against heat loss. During the night, when heat is required in the greenhouse, cool air from inside the greenhouse is forced through the rocks, where it is warmed and then passed back into the greenhouse. A clear polyethylene tube with holes along either side serves well to distribute the warm air uniformly along the length of the greenhouse. Conventional convection tubes can be used for distributing solar heated air. The water or rock storage unit occupies a large amount of space and a considerable amount of insulation is provided when the unit is placed outside. Placing it inside the greenhouse offers an advantage in that escaping heat is beneficial during heating periods, but it is detrimental when heating is not required. Rock beds can pose a problem in that they must remain relatively dry. Water evaporating from these beds will remove considerable heat.

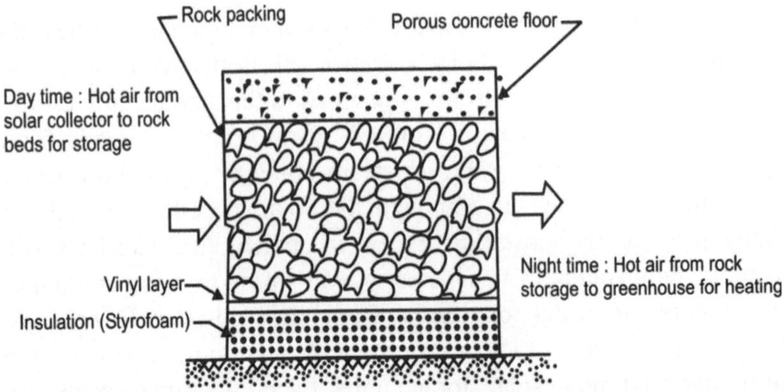

Fig. 12.3 Cross section of a typical rock storage unit.

12.6 Heat Conservation Practices

Energy can be saved significantly in a greenhouse if a grower implements the following suggestions of the American Council for Agricultural Science and Technology (CAST, 1975):

1. Tighten up the house, closing all possible openings.
2. Use polyethylene or fiberglass on the inside of gable ends.
3. Maintain the steam or hot water system regularly to stop leaks.
4. Use reflector materials behind heating pipes to reflect heat into the greenhouse.
5. Maintain the boiler at peak efficiency.
6. Insulate hot water and steam supply and return piping, and inspect at intervals, replacing the insulation when needed.
7. Maintain the automatic valves in the heating system, and
8. Check the thermostats regularly for proper operation.

The following are the other improved practices for energy conservation:

1. Covering a greenhouse with a double layer of polyethylene to reduce the loss of heat energy.

2. Placing a removable sheet of polyethylene over the crop and a row cover over each plant row in order to reduce heat loss from the greenhouse during night.
3. Application of opaque sheets as curtains during night.
4. Application of at least one layer of movable thermal screen.
5. Polyethylene tubing installed which, when inflated, seals the growing area from the roof surface area.
6. Improved curtain materials with greater reflective property conserve more energy.

12.7 Heat Requirement Calculation

The calculation of heat required for heating greenhouses was based on the sum of the quantities of heat lost through different structural components of greenhouses in unit time. Shapes of greenhouse (A-frame and quonset) alter the nature of greenhouse structural components (roof, wall, gable, curtain wall, curved covering and end) and hence influence the calculation of heat requirement (Fig. 12.3). Even though the heat loss occurs through conduction, convection and radiation, simpler heat loss calculations consider the combined heat loss. Standard heat loss values across components of different types of greenhouses and conversion factors to cover various conditions are available (Table 12.1-12.6). Combined heat loss values given in Tables 12.1, 12.2 and 12.6 were actually derived at standard conditions (39°C and 6.7 m/s) which can be modified to suit various prevailing conditions by using the conversion factors of Tables 12.3, 12.4 and 12.5. Based on calculated heat requirement, the fuel quantity required to provide the heat can also be estimated.

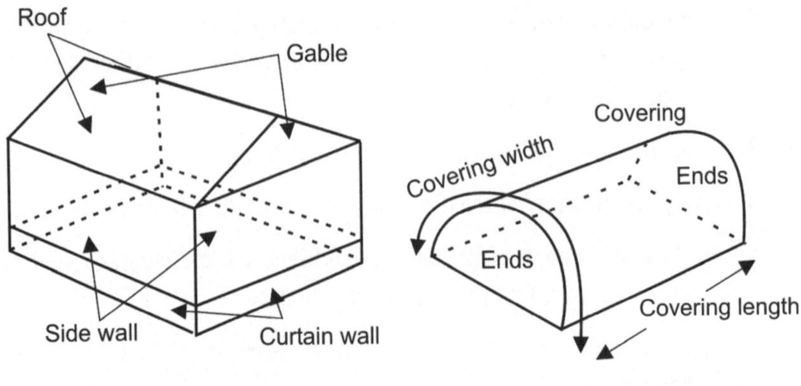

(a) A-Frame greenhouse (b) Quonset greenhouse

Fig. 12.4 Greenhouse structural components of heat requirement calculations.

12.7.1 Heat Requirement of A-frame Greenhouse

For A-frame greenhouse (Fig.12.3a), the heating requirement is calculated as follows:

1. It will be convenient to make a tabular form for the heat loss requirement, depicting different components involved, standard heat loss through components, correction factors and corrected heat loss values.
2. Estimate the combined standard heat loss through gables and roofs (Table 12.1).
3. Estimate the standard heat loss through sidewalls and curtain walls by considering them simply as walls having length based on greenhouse perimeter and with appropriate height (Table 12.2).
4. Determine the climatic factor (*K*) using the existing temperature difference and wind velocity (Table 12.3), construction factor (*C*) based on the type of greenhouse (Table 12.4), and curtain-wall construction factor (*CW*) (Table 12.5).
5. Apply appropriate *K*, *C* or *CW* factors to the standard heat loss values to get the corrected heat loss values for the existing conditions.

Table 12.1 Standard heat-loss values for A-frame greenhouses gables and roofs.

Greenhouse length in m (ft)	Greenhouse width in m (ft)														
	4.9 (16)	5.5 (18)	6.1 (20)	6.7 (22)	7.3 (24)	7.9 (26)	8.5 (28)	9.1 (30)	9.8 (32)	10.4 (34)	11.0 (36)	11.6 (36)	12.2 (40)	15.2 (50)	18.3 (60)
	Gable loss both sides in kW - independent of length														
	1.465	1.758	2.345	2.931	3.224	3.810	4.396	5.275	5.861	6.741	7.620	8.499	9.378	14.654	21.101
	Roof loss both sides in kW														
1.5 (5)	2.051	2.345	2.638	2.931	3.224	3.517	3.517	3.810	4.103	4.386	4.689	4.982	5.275	6.448	7.620
3.0 (10)	4.103	4.689	5.275	5.568	6.154	6.741	7.327	7.913	8.206	8.792	9.378	9.964	10.257	13.188	15.826
6.1 (20)	8.206	9.378	10.257	11.430	12.309	13.481	14.654	15.533	16.705	17.584	18.757	19.636	20.808	25.790	31.066
9.1 (30)	12.309	14.067	15.533	16.998	18.757	20.222	21.687	23.446	24.911	26.376	28.135	29.600	31.066	38.978	46.891
12.2 (40)	16.705	18.757	20.808	22.860	24.911	26.963	29.014	31.066	33.117	35.169	37.220	39.565	41.616	51.874	62.131
15.2 (50)	20.808	23.446	26.083	28.428	31.066	33.703	36.341	38.978	41.616	44.254	46.258	49.236	51.874	65.062	77.957
18.3 (60)	24.911	28.135	31.066	34.289	37.220	40.444	43.668	46.598	49.822	53.046	55.977	59.200	62.131	77.664	93.197
21.3 (70)	29.014	32.824	36.341	39.858	43.668	47.184	50.701	54.511	58.028	61.838	65.355	68.872	72.682	90.852	109.022
24.4 (80)	33.117	37.220	41.616	45.719	49.822	53.925	58.028	62.131	66.527	70.630	74.733	78.836	82.939	103.747	124.262
27.4 (90)	37.220	41.909	46.598	51.287	55.977	60.666	65.355	70.044	74.733	79.422	84.111	88.801	93.490	116.642	140.088
30.5 (100)	41.616	46.598	51.874	57.149	62.131	67.406	72.682	77.957	82.939	88.214	93.490	98.472	103.747	129.830	155.914
61.0 (200)	82.939	93.490	103.747	114.298	124.555	134.813	145.363	155.624	166.171	176. 429	186.686	197.237	207.494	259.368	311.242
91.4 (300)	124.555	140.088	155.621	171.154	186.686	202.219	217.752	233.578	249.110	264.643	280.176	295.709	311.242	389.198	467.155
121.9 (400)	165.878	186.686	207.494	228.302	249.110	269.625	290.433	311.242	332.050	352.858	373.373	394.181	414.989	518.736	622.483
152.4 (500)	207.494	233.578	259.368	285.451	311.242	337.032	363.115	389.198	415.282	441.072	466.862	492.946	518.736	648.566	781-328

Note : Values based on standard condition of 39 °C temperature difference between inside and outside and 6.7 m/s average wind velocity

Source : Bohanon, Rahilly and Stout (1993)

Table 12.2 Standard heat-loss values for greenhouse walls.

Greenhouse length in m (ft)	Heat loss values for wall height in m (ft)						
	0.61 (2)	**1.22 (4)**	**1.83 (6)**	**2.44 (8)**	**3.05 (10)**	**3.66 (12)**	**4.27 (14)**
	Wall loss in kW						
1.5 (5)	0.293	0.586	0.586	0.879	1.172	1.465	1.758
3.0 (10)	0.586	0.879	1.465	1.758	2.345	2.931	3.224
6.1 (20)	0.879	1.758	2.638	3.810	4.689	5.568	6.448
9.1 (30)	1.465	2.638	4.103	5.568	7.034	8.499	9.964
12.2 (40)	1.758	3.810	5.568	7.620	9.378	11.137	13.188
15.2 (50)	2.345	4.689	7.034	9.378	11.723	14.067	16.412
18.3 (60)	2.638	5.568	8.206	11.137	13.774	16.998	19.636
21.3 (70)	3.224	6.448	9.671	12.895	16.119	19.636	22.860
24.4 (80)	3.810	7.327	11.137	14.947	18.463	22.566	26.376
27.4 (90)	4.103	8.206	12.602	16.998	20.808	25.204	29.600
30.5 (100)	4.689	9.378	13.774	18.757	23.153	28.135	32.824
61.0 (200)	9.378	18.463	27.842	37.513	46.305	56.270	65.648
91.4 (300)	13.774	27.842	41.616	56.270	69.458	84.404	98.472
121.9 (400)	18.463	37.220	55.684	75.026	92.610	112.539	131.296
152.4 (500)	23.153	46.305	69.458	93.783	115.763	140.674	164.120

Source : Bohanon, Rahilly and Stout (1993)

Table 12.3 Climatic factor (*K*) for various average wind velocity and temperature conditions.

Inside-to-outside temperature difference (°C)	Climatic factor (*K*) for wind velocity in m/s				
	6.7	**8.9**	**11.2**	**13.4**	**15.6**
16.7	0.41	0.43	0.46	0.48	0.50
19.4	0.48	0.50	0.53	0.55	0.57
22.2	0.55	0.57	0.60	0.62	0.64
25.0	0.62	0.65	0.67	0.70	0.72
27.8	0.69	0.72	0.74	0.77	0.80
30.6	0.77	0.80	0.83	0.86	0.89
33.3	0.84	0.88	0.91	0.94	0.98
36.1	0.92	0.96	0.99	1.03	1.07
38.9	1.00	1.04	1.08	1.12	1.16
41.7	1.08	1.12	1.17	1.21	1.25
44.4	1.16	1.21	1.26	1.30	1.35
47.2	1.25	1.30	1.35	1.40	1.45
50.0	1.33	1.38	1.44	1.49	1.54

Source: Bohanon, Rahilly and Stout (1993)

Table 12.4 Greenhouse construction factor (*C*) for the common types of greenhouses.

Type of greenhouse	*C*
All metal (tight glass house – 0.51 or 0.61 m glass width)	1.08
Wood and steel (tight glass house – 0.41 or 0.51 m glass width – metal gutters, vents, headers etc.)	1.05
Wood house (glass with wooden bars, gutters, vents, etc. – up to and including 0.51 m glass spacing	1.05
Good tight house	1.00
Fairly tight house	1.13
Loose house	1.25
FRP–covered wood house	0.95
FRP-covered metal house	1.00
Double glass with 25 mm air space	0.70
Plastic-covered metal house (single thickness)	1.00
Plastic-covered metal house (double thickness)	0.70
Corrugated single-layer polycarbonate on wood	0.95
Corrugated single-layer polycarbonate on metal	1.00
Acrylic or polycarbonate twin-wall panel 8 mm thick	0.65
Acrylic or polycarbonate twin-wall panel 16 mm thick	0.58
Polycarbonate triple-wall panel 8 mm thick	0.50

Source : Bohanon, Rahilly and Stout (1993) and Nelson (2003)

Table 12.5 Greenhouse curtain-wall construction factor (*CW*) for the common types.

Type of material	*CW*
Glass	1.13
Asbestos-cement	1.15
Concrete, 0.1 m	0.78
Concrete, 0.2 m	0.58
Concrete block, 0.1 m	0.64
Concrete block, 0.2 m	0.51

Source: National Greenhouse Manufacturers Association (2004)

Table 12.6 Standard heat-loss values for quonset-type greenhouses combined ends and entire covering along the length.

Greenhouse length in m (ft)	Covering width in m (ft)											
	5.5 (18)	6.1 (20)	6.7 (22)	7.3 (24)	7.9 (26)	8.5 (28)	9.1 (30)	9.8 (32)	10.4 (34)	11.0 (36)	11.6 (36)	12.2 (40)
	Covering width in m (ft)											
	2.345	2.931	3.517	4.396	4.982	5.861	6.741	7.620	8.499	9.671	10.551	11.723
	Covering width in m (ft)											
1.5 (5)	2.051	2.345	2.638	2.638	2.931	3.224	3.517	3.810	3.810	4.103	4.396	4.689
3.0 (10)	4.103	4.689	4.982	5.568	6.154	6.448	7.0.34	7.327	7.913	8.206	8.792	9.378
6.1 (20)	8.206	9.378	10.257	11.137	12.016	12.895	13.774	14.947	15.826	16.705	17.584	18.463
9.1 (30)	12.602	13.774	15.240	16.705	18.170	19.343	20.808	22.273	23.739	24.911	26.376	27.842
12.2 (40)	16.705	18.463	20.515	22.273	24.032	26.083	27.842	29.600	30.186	33.410	35.169	37.220
15.2 (50)	20.808	23.153	25.497	27.842	30.186	32.531	34.875	37.220	39.272	41.616	43.961	46.305
18.3 (60)	24.911	27.842	30.479	33.410	36.048	38.978	41.616	44.547	47.184	50.115	52.753	55.684
21.3 (70)	29.307	32.531	35.755	38.978	42.202	45.426	48.650	51.874	55.097	58.321	61.838	65.062
24.4 (80)	33.410	37.220	40.737	44.547	48.064	51.874	55.684	59.200	63.010	66.820	70.337	74.147
27.4 (90)	37.513	41.616	46.012	50.115	54.218	58.321	62.717	66.820	70.923	75.026	79.422	83.525
30.5 (100)	41.616	46.305	50.994	55.684	60.373	64.769	69.458	74.147	78.836	83.525	88.214	92.610
61.0 (200)	83.525	92.610	101.989	111.367	120.452	129.830	139.209	148.294	157.672	167. 051	176. 136	185.514
91.4 (300)	124.141	139.209	152.983	166.757	180.825	194.599	208.667	222.441	236.508	250.283	264.350	278.124
121.9 (400)	167.051	185.514	203.977	222.441	240.904	259.661	278.124	296.588	315.051	333.808	352.271	370.735
152.4 (500)	208.667	231.819	254.972	278.124	301.277	324.430	347.875	370.735	394.181	417.333	440.486	463.638

Note ; Values based on standard condition of 39 °C temperature difference between inside and outside and 6.7 m/s average wind velocity.

Source : Bohanon, Rahilly and stout (1993)

6. Determine total heat loss by adding all the corrected heat losses.

7. When the heat source (heater, burner or boiler) was located outside the greenhouse, losses during heat transport should also be added to the total heat requirement. If overhead heater and wall heating coils were the heat sources, these units should share the heat requirement based on their contribution.

8. Based on heating values and thermal efficiencies of fuels, the quantity of fuel required to supply the total heat requirement are estimated.

Heating values and thermal efficiencies of some of the common fuels used in greenhouse heating calculation are shown in Table 12.7.

Table 12.7 Fuel heating value and thermal efficiency of common fuels

Type of material	*CW*
Fuel heating value:	
Anthracite coal	30 kJ/g
Semi-anthracite coal	32 kJ/g
Low-volatile bituminous coal	33.3 kJ/g
High-volatile bituminous coal	25-30.4 kJ/g
No. 1 fuel oil	31.7-38.2 kJ/ml
No. 2 fuel oil	37.9-39.6 kJ/ml
No. 4 fuel oil	39.3-42.8 kJ/ml
No. 5 fuel oil	41.3-43.5 kJ/ml
Natural gas	37300 kJ/m^3
Propane	95700 kJ/m^3
Green wood chips	10.5 kJ/g
Dried wood chips	19.8 kJ/g
Thermal efficiencies of fuels:	
Hard Coal	70%
Soft Coal	55%
Oil & Gas	85%
Wood	65%

Source : Nelson (2003)

Numerical Example 1

Determine the heat requirement for an all-metal glass greenhouse measuring 9.1 m wide by 30.5 m long. The curtain wall is 0.61 m high and is constructed of 0.1 m concrete block. The glass wall above the curtain wall is 1.83 m high. An average wind velocity of 6.7 m/s (24.1 km/h) is expected. A 33°C temperature difference is expected between the outside temperature of –17°C and the inside temperature of 16°C. Also calculate the fuel requirement for anthracite coal (heating value = 30 kJ/g, thermal efficiency = 70%) and for No. 2 fuel oil (heating value = 37.9 kJ/ml, thermal efficiency = 85%) (Nelson, 2003).

***Solution**:*

The step by step procedure involved in heat requirement calculation is as follows:

1. Prepare a heat loss table for the calculation (shown below).
2. Obtain the combined gable loss from Table 12.1 for a house of 9.1 m width as 5.275 kW. Note that the gable loss is independent of length of house, and the combined loss accounts for both the ends.
3. Obtain the combined roof loss from Table 12.1 for a house of 9.1 m wide and 30.5 m long as 77.957 kW. Combined loss value will take into account of both the roof slopes.
4. Heat loss through walls is based on the total wall length (perimeter). The perimeter of the house is 2 × (9.1 + 30.5) = 79.2 m. Heat loss for 1.83 m high wall with 79.2 m length from Table 12.2 is obtained by splitting the length as 18.3 + 61.0 m gives 8.206 + 27.842 kW = 36.048 kW.
5. Similarly, heat loss through the curtain wall of 0.61 m high and 79.2 m long from Table 12.2 is 2.638 + 9.378 kW = 12.016 kW.
6. Climatic factor (*K*) for an inside-to-outside temperature difference of 16 – (-17)°C = 33°C and average wind velocity of 6.7 m/s from Table 12.3 is 0.84. This factor is applicable to all greenhouse components.

7. Greenhouse construction factor (*C*) for an all-metal glass greenhouse from Table 12.4 is 1.08. This factor is applicable to all components made of glass i.e., gables, roof, and side walls except curtain walls.

8. Greenhouse curtain wall construction factor (*CW*) is obtained separately from Table 12.5, based on construction material. For a 0.10 m thick concrete block curtain wall, the *CW* factor is 0.64.

9. Input the heat loss values and correction factors in a tabular form and obtain the corrected heat loss by multiplying the quantities of each component as shown.

Greenhouse component	Standard heat loss (kW)	Climatic factor K	Construction factor C or *CW*	Corrected heat loss (kW)
Gables	5.275	0.84	1.08*	4.7855
Roof	77.957	0.84	1.08*	70.7226
Side walls	36.084	0.84	1.08*	32.7027
Curtain walls	12.016	0.84	0.64†	6.4598
Total heat requirement				**114.6706**

*Note: *-factor C, †-factor CW*

10. All heat could be provided by an overhead heating unit in a mild climate. In cold climatic conditions, wall heaters with pipe coils should provide the heat that was lost through the side and curtain walls (in this case: 32.7027 + 6.4598 kW = 39.1625 kW). The balance heat lost through gables and roof (in this case: 4.7855 + 70.7226 kW = 75.5081 kW) should be taken care by the overhead heating system.

11. Fuel consumption could be calculated from the heating value and thermal efficiency of the selected fuels from Table 12.7.

For anthracite coal

$$= \frac{114.6706(\text{kJ}/\text{s})}{30.0(\text{kJ}/\text{g}) \times 0.70} = 5.4605 \text{ g/s} = 19.66 \text{ kg/s}.$$

For No. 2 fuel oil

$$= \frac{114.6706(\text{kJ}/\text{s})}{37.9(\text{kJ}/\text{ml}) \times 0.85} = 3.5595 \text{ ml/s} = 12.81 \text{ 1/h}.$$

12.7.2 Heat Requirement of Quonset Greenhouse

Calculation of heat requirement for quonset greenhouse is similar to A-frame greenhouse, but the difference lies in the shape of the house that has only two structural components, such as covering and ends (Fig. 12.3b). The covering of quonset greenhouse is equivalent to combined roof and walls of A-frame greenhouse. Heat loss through ends and covering is found from Table 12. 6. For heat loss calculations, the covering width (curved) of house is considered, since it is possible to have different curved widths for a given ground width of house based on different central heights. Climatic (*K*) and construction factors (*C*) are obtained, as usual, using Tables 12.3, 12.4, and 12.5.

Numerical Example 2

Determine the heat requirement for a metal framed quonset greenhouse measuring 9.1 m wide by 30.5 m long and covered with two layers of polyethylene, each measuring 12.2 m wide. A temperature difference of 33°C and an average wind velocity of 6.7 m/s (24.1 km/h) are expected. Also calculate the fuel requirement for anthracite coal (heating value = 30 kJ/g, thermal efficiency = 70%) and No. 2 fuel oil (heating value = 37.9 kJ/ml, thermal efficiency = 85%) (Nelson, 2003).

Solution:

The step by step procedure involved in heat requirement calculation is as follows:

1. Prepare a heat loss table depicting different components and factors for the calculation (shown below).
2. Obtain the combined end loss from Table 12.6 for a house of 12.2 m covering width as 11.723 kW. Note the covering width is used in the calculation and the combined end loss is independent of house length.
3. Obtain the covering loss from Table 12.6 for a house of 12.2 m covering width and 30.5 m length as 92.610 kW.
4. Climatic factor (*K*) for an inside-to-outside temperature difference of 33°C and average wind velocity of 6.7 m/s from

Table 12.3 is 0.84. This factor is applicable to all greenhouse structural components.

5. Greenhouse construction factor (*C*) for a double layered plastic-covered metal greenhouse from Table 12.4 is 0.70. This factor is applicable to both ends and covering.

6. Complete the tabular form with heat loss values and correction factors and obtain the corrected heat loss by multiplying the quantities of each component as shown.

Greenhouse component	**Standard heat loss (kW)**	**Climatic factor K**	**Construction factor *C***	**Corrected heat loss (kW)**
Combined ends	11.723	0.84	0.70	6.8931
Covering	92.610	0.84	0.70	54.4547
Total heat requirement				**61.3478**

7. Fuel consumption could be calculated from the heating value and thermal efficiency of the selected fuels from Table 12.7.

For anthracite coal

$$= \frac{61.3478(\text{kJ/s})}{30.0(\text{kJ/g})/0.70} = 2.9213 \text{ g/s} = 10.52 \text{ kg/h}$$

For No.2 fuel oil

$$= \frac{61.3478(\text{kJ/s})}{37.9(\text{kJ/g})/0.85} = 1.9043 \text{ ml/s} = 6.86 \text{ l/h}$$

12.7.3 Simplified Method of Heat Requirement Calculation

Another simple and quick approach for calculating the heat requirements is based on heat transfer occurring across greenhouse defined by the overall heat transfer equation. The amount of heat lost from a greenhouse depends on 1. Glazing materials, 2. Exposed surface area of the house, 3. Inside desired temperature, 4. Outside existing temperature, 5. Wind speed, and 6. Condition of house (old, new, tight or loose). The outside temperature should be based on the lowest average expected temperature during the heating season.

The overall heat transfer equation for a greenhouse is given as:

$$Q = U \times A \times (T_i - T_o)$$

where Q is the overall transferred heat (W), U is the overall heat transfer coefficient for the material (W/m^2·°C), A is the exposed surface area of the structural material (m^2), T_i is the inside desired temperature (°C), and T_o is the outside temperature (°C).

Overall heat transfer equation, being simple in nature, accounts for the overall heat loss through the greenhouse structural material at general conditions, and will not account for losses due to excessive wind velocities, loose fittings, or ventilation. To account for these losses, an additional 10% can be added to the calculated total heat. The overall heat transfer coefficient (U) value should be varying with structural materials (glazing and curtain wall), and weather conditions. Exposed heat transfer surface area (A) can be calculated from the geometry of greenhouse.

The U-values (W/m^2·°C) of typical greenhouse glazing materials (ASAE Standards, 2002) are:

Type of material	***U***
Brick wall (varies with material, thickness, insulation, etc.)	2.5-3.7
Glass double pane	3.0
Acrylic and polycarbonate sheets	3.5
FRP	5.7
IR-absorbing and PVC film	5.7
UV-stabilized polyethylene films	6.3
Glass single pane	6.3

Numerical Example 3

Calculate the heat requirement for a metal framed glass greenhouse of 9.8 m wide by 30.5 m long and wall height of 1.8 m. The central height at the gable end above the wall is 2.74 m. Take the overall heat transfer coefficient U for glass is 6.53 W/m^2·°C. The desired inside and existing outside temperatures are 15.5°C and –17.8°C, respectively. (Boodley, 1996).

Solution:

Make a sketch of the greenhouse with the given dimensions as shown:

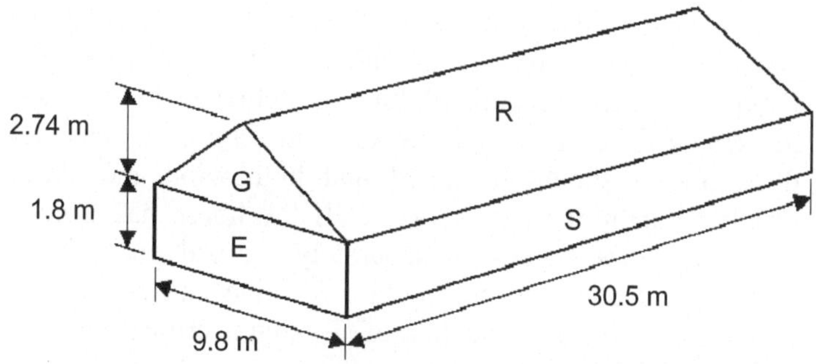

From the geometry of the greenhouse, calculate the area of each structural component as follows:

Area of end walls (**E**)

$$= 9.8 \text{ m} \times 1.8 \text{ m} \times 2 \text{ (two end walls)} = 35.28 \text{ m}^2$$

Area of side walls (**S**)

$$= 30.5 \text{ m} \times 1.8 \text{ m} \times 2 \text{ (two side walls)} = 109.8 \text{ m}^2$$

Area of gable ends (**G**) based on area of triangle

$$= \tfrac{1}{2} \times 9.8 \text{ m} \times 2.74 \text{ m} \times 2 \text{ (two gable ends)} = 26.85 \text{ m}^2$$

The inclined length of the roof (rafter length) can be calculated from the geometry of right angled triangle from the sketch as

$$\text{Inclined length of roof} = \sqrt{(9.8/2)^2 + 2.74^2} = 5.61 \text{ m}$$

Area of roofs (**R**) based on their inclined length and length of greenhouse

$$= 5.61 \text{ m} \times 30.5 \text{ m} \times 2 \text{ (two roof slopes)} = 342.21 \text{ m}^2$$

Hence, the total exposed area of heat transfer (A)

$$= 35.28 + 109.8 + 26.85 + 342.21 \text{ m}^2$$

$$= 514.14 \text{ m}^2$$

Substituting in overall heat transfer equation

Heat requirement (Q)

$$= 6.53\ \text{W/m}^2{\cdot}°\text{C} \times 514.14\ \text{m}^2 \times (15.5 - (\ 17.8))°\text{C}$$

$$= 111799\ \text{W} = 112\ \text{kW}.$$

Hence, heaters should be selected with a net effective heating capacity of 112 kW. For greenhouses of 30.5 m length or longer, efficient heat distribution is achieved by two small heaters with total heating capacity matching the calculated heat loss. It should be noted that high wind and extreme weather conditions alter U-value. If the house had a curtain wall, heat loss should be separately worked out using the curtain wall area and appropriate U-value and added to the total loss. Hence, the selection of U-value is critical for a good estimate of heat requirement.

Numerical Example 4

Calculate the heat requirement for a double layered polyethylene arch roof greenhouse of 9.8 m wide by 30.5 m long and wall height of 1.8 m. The central height at the circular arc hoop above the wall is 2.74 m. Take the overall heat transfer coefficient U for double layer polyethylene as *4.543 W/m²·°C. The desired inside and existing outside temperatures are 15.5°C and -17.8°C, respectively.*

Solution:

Make a sketch of the greenhouse with the given dimensions as shown:

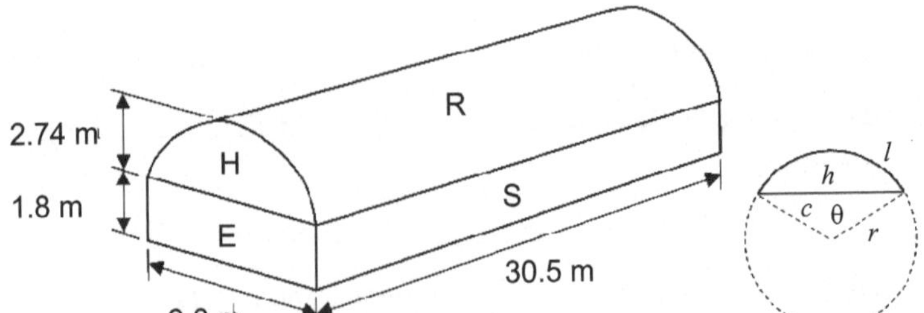

From the geometry of the greenhouse, calculate the area of each structural component as follows:

Area of end walls (**E**) = 9.8 m × 1.8 m × 2 (two end walls)

$$= 35.28\ \text{m}^2$$

Area of side walls (**S**) = 30.5 m × 1.8 m × 2 (two side walls)

= 109.8 m^2

Arch section was assumed as a portion of circular arc (refer sketch) with greenhouse width as chord length (c) and height of arch at the middle (the maximum height of the arc from the cord) above the wall (h). For the arc portion above the chord, consider the length of the arc as l, the radius of the arc as r, subtended angle in radians as θ and S as the enclosed area of the arc. From standard geometrical formula of segment of circle

(http://mathforum.org/dr.math/faq/faq.circle.segment.html#8)

$$r = \frac{c^2 + 4h^2}{8h}$$

$$\theta = 2 \times \arcsin\left(\frac{c}{2r}\right)$$

$$l = r \times \theta$$

$$S = \frac{r^2}{2}(\theta - \sin\theta)$$

Substituting the values in the above equations:

r = (9.82^2 m^2 + 4 × 2.74^2 m^2) / (8 × 2.74 m) = 5.75 m

θ = 2 × arcsin [9.8 m /(2 × 5.75 m)] = 2.039 radian

l = 5.75 m × 2.039 = 11.73 m

S = (5.75^2 m^2 / 2) × [2.039 – sin(2.039)] = 18.96 m^2

Area of arch portions (**H**) based on the contained area (S)

= 18.96 m^2 × 2 (two arch ends) = 37.92 m^2

Area of arch roof (**R**) based on the arc length (l)

= 11.73 m × 30.5 m ×1 (whole arch length) = 357.77 m^2

Hence the total exposed area of heat transfer (A)

= 35.28 + 109.8 + 37.92 + 357.77 m^2 = 540.77 m^2

Substituting in overall heat transfer equation, the heat requirement is

$$Q = 4.543 \text{ W/m}^2\cdot°\text{C} \times 540.77 \text{ m}^2 \times (15.5 - (-17.8))\ °\text{C}$$

$$= 81809 \text{ W} = 82 \text{ kW}.$$

Hence, a heater with net effective capacity of 82 kW should be chosen. For efficient heat distribution, two small heaters having this combined capacity can be selected.

Superior insulation effect of double layer polyethylene glazing than glass as observed from the examples (3 and 4) is because of the entrapped air, which acts as a good heat insulator and produces a relatively reduced *U*-value (more resistance to heat flow). Therefore, good savings in the heating requirement can be achieved with double layer of polyethylene, as the single layer polyethylene or fiber glass glazing material has nearly the same *U*-value as glass.

Arch roof geometry will be more simplified if the arch is a semi-circle. Quonset type greenhouses can be visualized as direct segment of circles without the straight wall portion, as found in arch type houses. The geometrical analyses were equally applicable in both cases of semi-circular arch and circular segment shaped quonset type greenhouses.

REVIEW QUESTIONS

1. What are the different modes of heat losses in greenhouse and the ways to arrest them?
2. Explain briefly the four types of greenhouse heating systems.
3. What are the two common methods of heat distribution systems?
4. Describe the horizontal air flow heat distribution system with suitable layout diagrams of different sizes of greenhouse.
5. Explain the solar heating system with a neat sketch.
6. Write a note with diagrams on the water and rock storage facility in greenhouse.

7. List the suggestions by the American Council for Agricultural Science and Technology for energy saving in greenhouse management.

8. Mention the other improved practices for energy conservation in greenhouse.

9. Estimate the heat requirement for an all-metal glass greenhouse measuring 15.2 m wide by 61.0 m long. The curtain wall is 0.61 m high and is constructed of 20 cm concrete block. The glass wall above the curtain wall is 2.44 m high. An average wind velocity of 6.7 m/s is expected. A 31°C temperature difference is expected between the outside low temperature of –13 °C and the inside temperature of 18°C. Determine the fuel requirement for bituminous coal (heating value = 33 kJ/g, thermal efficiency = 55 %) and No. 4 fuel oil (heating value = 39.3 kJ/ml, thermal efficiency = 85%).

   [Answer: Total heat requirement = 314.9588 W; Bituminous coal requirement = 62.47 kg/h; No. 4 fuel oil requirement = 33.94 l/h]

10. Estimate the heat requirement for a metal framed semicircular quonset greenhouse of 6.1 m wide by 24.4 m long and covered with two layers of polyethylene, each having a covering width of 9.8 m. A temperature difference of 25°C and an average wind velocity of 11.2 m/s are expected. Determine the fuel requirement for bituminous coal (heating value = 33 kJ/g, thermal efficiency = 55 %) and No. 4 fuel oil (heating value = 39.3 kJ/ml, thermal efficiency = 85%).

    [Answer: Total heat requirement = 31.3386 W; Bituminous coal requirement = 6.22 kg/h; No. 4 fuel oil requirement = 3.38 l/h]

11. Calculate the heat requirement for a metal A-framed glass greenhouse of 5.0 m wide by 20 m long and wall height of 1.6 m. The central height at the gable end above the wall is 1.5 m. Take the overall heat transfer coefficient U for glass is 6.3 W/m^2 °C. The desired inside is 16°C and existing outside temperature is 1.5°C.

    [Answer: Areas E = 16.0, S = 64.0, G = 7.5, R = 116.8, A = 204.3m^2; Heat requirement = 18663 W]

12. Calculate the heat requirement for a double layered polyethylene quonset type greenhouse of 8 m wide by 24 m long. The central height of the hoop from ground level is above the wall is 3.5 m. The desired inside and existing outside temperatures are 15°C and 1°C, respectively. The overall heat transfer coefficient U for double layer polyethylene is 4.5 $W/m^2 \cdot °C$. Also determine the fuel requirement for No. 2 fuel oil (heating value = 37.9. kJ/ml, thermal efficiency = 85%).
[Answer: r = 4.04 m; _ = 2.86 radian; l = 11.55 m; S = 21.07 m^2; H = 42.14 m^2; R = 277.2 m^2; A = 319.34 m^2; Heat requirement = 20118 W; Fuel oil requirement = 2.25 l/h]

Chapter 13

ENVIRONMENTAL REQUIREMENTS FOR CROPS AND PEST CONTROL

Growing greenhouse vegetables is one of the most exacting and intensive forms of all agriculture enterprises. In the controlled environment of a greenhouse, high yields of excellent quality vegetables can be produced. A successful greenhouse grower should have a good knowledge of agriculture, horticulture, soils, plant pathology, entomology, and plant physiology, as well as the engineering capability to provide an environment best suited for plant growth. The important environmental factors that affect the horticultural crops inside the greenhouse are temperature, light, relative humidity, and CO_2 concentration. Classification of horticultural crops is also made based on the optimum temperature and lighting conditions for better growth. Direct effect of temperature and the differential day and night temperature controls the overall growth of the plants. The components of light that affect the production are intensity, quality, and duration. Relative humidity of air is a measure of the moisture available in air, and it has good correlation to the occurrence of pest and diseases. The frightening ability of some insects to develop resistance to chemical pesticides has revived worldwide interest in the concept of biological control. Enclosure of the growing area makes it easier for the controlling operations in greenhouse than in open field agriculture. This chapter deals with the environmental requirement of horticultural crops, light requirement and its control, floricultural crops, pests and disease control, and the integrated pest management inside greenhouse.

13.1 Temperature Requirements of Horticultural Crops

Of all the climatic factors affecting the vegetable production, temperature is considered to be the most important factor. Temperature affects the germination, flowering, pollination, fruit-set, quality of produce and seed production. Based on temperature requirements, vegetable crops in general are classified into:

1. Cool season crops that survive at temperatures ranging from 0 to 10°C (Garden beans, broad beans, carrots, cauliflower, potato, peas, and lettuce).
2. Warm season crops can survive in the temperature range of 15 to 30°C (Cowpea, cucurbits, bell pepper, tomato, chillies, okra, and sweet potato).

Temperature variations affect the development of the economic parts of many crops. The optimum temperature range varies with crop and with its growth stage. Environmental requirements for some of the horticultural and floricultural crops are given in Table 13.1. Plant height can be controlled by adjusting the day-to-night temperature difference (DIF). The term DIF (acronym for the temperature differential) refers to the temperature difference obtained by subtracting the night temperature from the day temperature. The rate of stem internode elongation increases with the increase in day temperatures and with the decrease in night temperatures. Hence, the plants become tall when the DIF value is highly positive. Large reductions in plant height are achieved by reducing DIF from positive to zero values or negative values. The concept of DIF works well when plants are young and their rate of growth is rapid.

Table 13.1 Environmental Requirements for Some Horticultural and Floricultural Crops.

Crop	Season	Temperature (°C)	Relative humidity (%)	Light (klux)	Remarks
Potato	Sprouting and initial growth	20 to 24	-	-	Above 30°C
	Growth and tuberation	18 to 20	-	-	No tuber formation
Tomato	Fruit setting	21 to 30	-	-	CO_2 200 ppm
	Colour development (red and yellow)	10 to 30	-	-	-
Bell pepper	-	21 to 23	-	-	-
Onion	Bulb formation	20 to 22	-	-	-
Carrot	Root development	15 to 21	-	-	-
	Colour development	15 to 22	-	-	-
Cauliflower	Curd formation	17	-	-	-
Garlic, Brinjal, Pumpkins	-	-	-	-	Cool temperature
Vegetable seeds	Normal storage (conditions at different temperature and RH)	26 21 7	5 to 10 7 to 13 9 to 15	- - -	- - -
Mango	-	24 to 27	>80	-	-
Citrus	-	25	-	-	-
Banana	-	20 to 35	-	-	-
Passion fruit	-	20 to 30	-	-	-
Rose	-	13.3 to 21	-	64.6 to 86.1	CO_2, 1200 to 2000 ppm
Orchids	Day Night	15.5 to 21 10 to 15.5	> 30 > 80	25.8 to 38.7	CO_2 500 ppm
Gladiolus	-	15 to 25	15	-	-
Carnation	-	15.5 to 20	60 to 75	-	-
Chrysanthemum	-	8 to 12	-	-	-

13.2 Light Requirements of Crops and Lighting Control Methods

The performance of crops is influenced by the three aspects of light, namely, intensity, quality, and duration. Light intensity refers to the number of photons falling on a given area or the total amount of light which plants receive. Light intensity is specified in lux for each crop. A range of 32.3 to 86.1 klux is required by crops like cucurbits, capsicum, eggplant, and sweet potato, while cabbage, and sweet potato require 21.5 to 86.1 klux. Light quality refers to the wavelengths of the radiation. Composition of visible light affects the photosynthetic activity of plants. Length of the day is responsible for accumulation of carbohydrates and for flower induction in certain plants. Light duration plays an important role in photoperiodism, which is the response of an organism to the day-night cycle.

The relative length of the light and dark periods governs a number of responses including flowering, leaf shape, stem elongation, bulb formation and pigmentation. Based on the response of the plant to the light periods, plants are classified into long-day plants (requiring 8 to 10 h of continuous dark periods), short-day plants (requiring 10 to 14 h of continuous dark periods) and day-neutral plants (photo insensitive plants). Cucurbits, cowpea, lettuce, radish, pea, turnip, clover, and spinach are long-day plants; certain cultivars of cowpea, beans, onions, coffee, strawberry, and sweet potato are short-day plants; and cucumber, tomato, potato, and rose are day-neutral plants. The optimum light requirement varies with crops based on its classification (Table 13.1). Artificial shading and supplemental lighting systems can effectively control the plant photoperiodism and DIF in the greenhouse, which can be manipulated to the advantage of the growers.

13.2.1 Greenhouse Shading Methods

There is an established need for reducing light intensity in the bright sunshine months from May to August. This may be accomplished either by spraying a shading compound on the greenhouse, or by installing a screen fabric over the greenhouse or inside the greenhouse above head light. Commercial shading compounds can be directly purchased or made by mixing white latex paint with water. One part paint in 10 parts or water provides a very heavy shade, while one part paint in 15 to 20 parts water provides a standard shade. The shading compound can be sprayed on from the ground by means of a pesticide sprayer. Most of the shading compound will wear off by the end of the next season. When shade is desired only to protect flowers, sheets of screening are sometimes used only where they are needed. Cheesecloth was commonly used earlier and is still used when it offers a price advantage. Longer lasting synthetic fabrics are more popular today, including such material as polypropylene, polyester, saran, and aluminium coated polyester. The shade values of the former three can vary from 20 to 90%, although 50% is commonly used.

The problem with spraying shading compounds or installing a fixed sunscreen in the greenhouse is that the barrier will cause periods of inadequate light intensity leading to reduced growth and delayed crops, when the light intensity is low on cloudy days and in early morning or late afternoon on all days. Modern greenhouses have automated equipment to draw sunscreens across the greenhouse in response to photocell sensors. In this way, screening is applied only during the hours when it is needed. If the sunscreens are judiciously selected, they can also serve as thermal blankets for retaining heat on winter nights. The same apparatus used for drawing the screens in the daytime during the bright months can be used for drawing them during the nights in winter.

13.2.2 Greenhouse Supplemental Lighting Systems

Supplemental lighting during the daylight hours to enhance photosynthesis is proved to be highly effective. Such lighting is more profitable in high density plantings, such as rooting and seedling beds and the production of young plants. Many types of lamps have been used in the greenhouse. Basically, they fall into three groups:

1. Incandescent.
2. Fluorescent.
3. High-intensity-discharge (HID) such as high-pressure mercury, metal halide, low-pressure sodium and high-pressure sodium.

Tungsten filament incandescent lamps are generally not used for supplemental lighting because of poor light quality and excessive heat production. Fluorescent lamps are most commonly used in growing rooms and over small germination areas in the greenhouse. Now-a-days, the HID lamps are preferred types for the final stages of the crop growth in the greenhouse. The most commonly used HID system at present utilizes high-pressure sodium lamps. Supplemental lighting is used for most crops but is particularly popular with chrysanthemum and geranium stock plants, Elatior begonia, rose, and plug seedlings. Light intensities of 3.2 to 6.5 klux at plant height are generally used for seedlings and ornamental plants, with 4.3 klux being the most common level. Intensities of 6.5 to 10.8 klux are used for vegetable crops.

13.3 Floricultural Crops

Flowers have been important for three main considerations, namely, aesthetic, economic, and social. As with vegetable production, the growing of floricultural crops in greenhouses involves high technology and often capital intensive. Every floricultural crop has its own specific cultural and management requirements, which include stock plant management, propagation, nutrition, light intensity and duration, temperature, CO_2, irrigation, water quality, crop scheduling and pest control, along with other cultural practices. The greenhouse designs and environment control systems are basically like those systems used in greenhouse vegetable production, except growing benches are common in floriculture production and not in vegetable production (Fig. 13.1). The environmental requirements for few floricultural crops are also presented in Table 13.1.

Fig. 13.1 Flowers production on benches inside greenhouse.

13.4 Pest and Disease Control

Most disease and insect species are common throughout the world. Although some are specific to certain regions, in general, the problems and challenges are similar. It is common to assume that protected agriculture systems are relatively free of plant diseases and insect pests because the system is mostly enclosed. But pathogens and pests may be introduced when greenhouse doors are open and also through the people and materials. Most horticultural crops are susceptible to root diseases. There are several common root fungal diseases, while some fungi are specific to certain crops, bacteria, and nematodes cause other root diseases. The common fungal diseases are caused by *Fusarium, Verticillium, Pythium* and *Rhizoctonia* species. No foliage damaging plant diseases or insect pests associated exclusively with any system of protected agriculture. Some diseases and insects infect any crop, whether grown in the open field or under row covers or within a greenhouse. The common foliage diseases include viruses and several other bacterial and fungal diseases. Insects, common the world over, are aphids, whitefly, fungus gnats, shore flies, thrips, mealy bugs, and caterpillars. A protected environment is ideal for the rapid proliferation of unwanted pathogens and insects. Greenhouse operations are normally free of pests for several crops after initial construction, but always become infested after a period of operation. The different methods of pest and disease control include:

1. Weed control in and around the greenhouse.
2. Sanitation, cleaning and pasteurization prior to crop establishment.
3. Inspection and cleanup of newly acquired plants.
4. Screening of greenhouse entrances.
5. Routine surveillance for identification and quantification of pest appearances in the greenhouses as well as accurate recording of the same.
6. Adjustment of environmental conditions to render them suppressive to the pests at hand but not to the crop.
7. Pest eradication methods consisting of either biological control or pesticide application.

13.5 Integrated Pest Management

Integrated pest management (IPM) generally consists or a carefully structured and monitored combination of biological controls, plant genetics, cultural practices and use of chemicals. IPM guidelines are that insects can be controlled largely by encouraging their natural predators and parasites, by using resistant cultivars, and by using proper plant spacing and other cultural practices, and by using pesticides only as a last resort. IPM is also environmentally sound since it minimizes the dispersion of toxic materials and is consistent with the current interest in the consumption of natural foods.

Biological control involves the release of predator insects, parasite insects and related organisms, or pathogenic microorganisms into the crop that seek out and destroy the pests. Several beneficial organisms are commercially available for use. In floriculture production, it is difficult to produce foliage free of insect damage while maintaining low populations of pest, predators and parasites. Therefore, biological control is not as common in floriculture as in vegetable production. In culture control, very close spacing of plants inhibits air circulation and light penetration; this fosters the growth of insect populations and restricts access to them. Wider spacing facilitates monitoring and control of insects, as does a general program of greenhouse sanitation of removing trash, dead plants and other debris that may shelter pests. A CEA lighting system as a physical control should be designed and placed to avoid insects into the greenhouses. Certain interior lights such as UV or yellow mercury vapour, act as insect traps. Objects painted with certain colours and sprayed with adhesive materials serve as traps for some pests.

In the area of genetic control, cultivars have been developed for tolerance or resistance to certain insects, viruses, and fungi. Disease tolerance tomatoes have been a big boost to productivity, while the results were mixed in some resistant varieties of cucumbers. For the grower, a trade off may be necessary between yield potential and resistance. Selecting cultivars should be performed case by case, taking into account region, local pest population, and other factors. Chemical controls are used as a measure of last resort in an IPM program. This is more easily done in open field agriculture, with so many approved pesticides and chemical procedures; but difficult in CEA since so few chemicals are certified for greenhouse use. The severity of the residual problem is the reason for the non availability of many approved chemicals for CEA. Timeliness and uniformity of application of chemicals in CEA operations are crucial to the success of IPM programs. In IPM, by judicious use, amount of pesticides used can be greatly reduced.

REVIEW QUESTIONS

1. Define DIF, state its significance in controlling the plant height, and mention how it can be controlled in greenhouse.

2. Give the meaning and importance of the following terms:
   (a) Light intensity
   (b) Light quality
   (c) Photoperiodism
   (d) Long-day plants
   (e) Short-day plants
   (f) Day-neutral plants
3. Describe the methods of greenhouse shading.
4. Write an account on the supplemental lighting systems of greenhouse.
5. What are the general methods of greenhouse pest and disease control?
6. Discuss about integrated pest management with reference to greenhouse cultivation.

Chapter 14

GREENHOUSE IRRIGATION SYSTEMS

A well-designed irrigation system will supply the precise amount of water needed each day throughout the year. The quantity of water needed would depend on the growing area, the crop, weather conditions, the time of year and whether the heating or ventilation system is operating. Water needs are also dependent on the type of soil or soil mix and the size and type of the container or bed. Watering in the greenhouse most frequently accounts for loss in crop quality. Though the operation appears to be the simple, proper decision should be taken on how, when and what quantity to be given to the plants after continuous inspection and assessment. Since underwatering (less frequent) and overwatering (more frequent) will be injurious to the crops, the rules of watering should be strictly adhered to. Several irrigation water application systems, such as hand watering, perimeter watering, overhead sprinklers, boom watering, and drip irrigation which are currently in use will be discussed in this chapter.

14.1 Rules of Watering

The following are the three important rules of application of irrigation water.

Rule 1: Use a well-drained substrate with good structure

If the root substrate is not well drained and aerated, proper watering cannot be achieved. Hence substrates with ample moisture retention along with good aeration are indispensable for proper growth of the plants. The desired combination of coarse texture and highly stable structure can be obtained from the formulated substrates and not from field soil alone.

Rule 2: Water thoroughly each time

Partial watering of the substrates should be avoided; the supplied water should flow from the bottom in case of containers, and the root zone is wetted thoroughly in case of beds. As a rule, 10 to 15% excess of water is supplied. In general, the water requirement for soil based substrates is at a rate of 20 l/m^2 of bench, 0.3 to 0.35 l per 0.165 m diameter pot.

Rule 3: Water just before initial moisture stress occurs

Since overwatering reduces the aeration and root development, water should be applied just before the plant enters the early symptoms of water stress. The foliar symptoms, such as texture, colour, and turgidity can be used to determine the moisture stresses, but they vary with crops. For crops that do not show any symptoms, colour. Feel and weight of the substrates are used for assessment.

14.2 Hand Watering

The most traditional method of irrigation is hand watering and in present days is uneconomical. Growers can afford hand watering only where a crop is still at a high density, such as in seed beds, or when they are watered at a few selected pots or areas that have dried sooner than others. In all cases, the labour saved will pay for the automatic system in less than one year. It soon will become apparent that this cost is too high. In addition to this deterrent to hand watering, there is a great risk of applying too little water or of waiting too long between waterings. Hand watering requires considerable time and is very boring. It is usually performed by inexperienced employees, who may be tempted to speed up the job or put it off to another time. Automatic watering is rapid and easy and is performed by the grower himself. Where hand watering is practiced, a water breaker should be used on the end of the hose. Such a device breaks the force of the water, permitting a higher flow rate without washing the root substrate out of the bench or pot. It also lessens the risk of disrupting the structure of the substrate surface.

14.3 Perimeter Watering

Perimeter watering system can be used for crop production in benches or beds. A typical system consists of a plastic pipe around the perimeter of a bench with nozzles that spray water over the substrate surface below the foliage (Fig. 14.1).

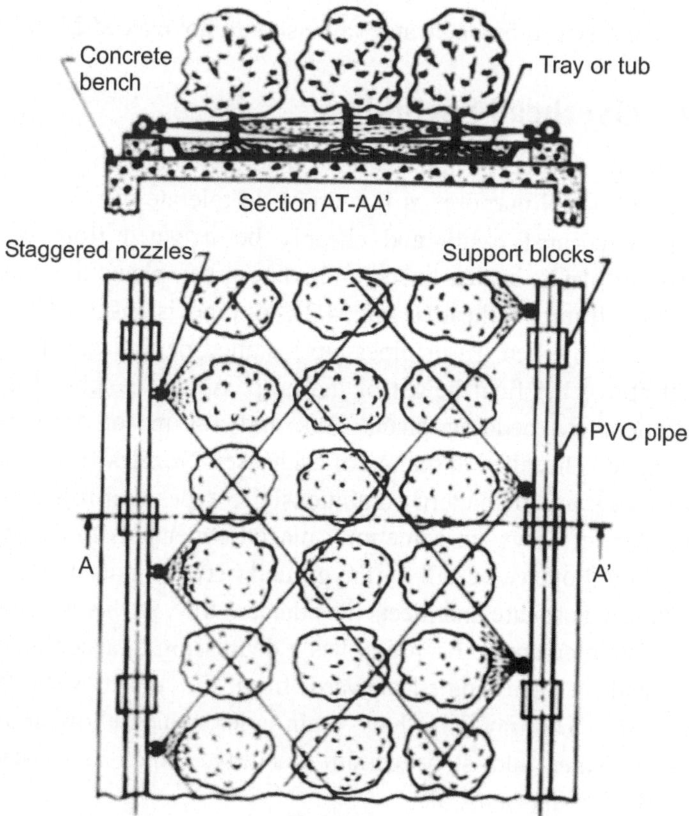

Fig. 14.1 Schematic diagram of perimeter watering system.

Either polyethylene or PVC pipe can be used. While PVC pipe has the advantage of being very stationary, polyethylene pipe tends to roll if it is not anchored firmly to the side of the bench. This causes nozzles to rise or fall from proper orientation to the substrate surface. Nozzles are made of nylon or a hard plastic and are available to put out a spray arc of 180°, 90° or 45°. Regardless of the types of nozzles used, they are staggered across the benches so that each nozzle projects out between two other nozzles on the opposite side. Perimeter watering systems with 180° nozzles require one water valve for benches up to 30.5 m in length. For benches over 30.5 m and up to 61.0 m, a water main should be installed on either side, one to serve each half of the bench. This system applies 1.25 l/min/m of pipe. Where 180° and 90° or 45° nozzles are alternated, the length of a bench serviced by one water valve should not exceed 23 m.

14.4 Overhead Sprinklers

While the foliage on the majority of crops should be kept dry for disease control purposes, a few crops do tolerate wet foliage. These crops can most easily and cheaply be irrigated from overhead. Bedding plants, azalea liners, and some green plants are commonly watered from overhead (Fig. 14.2). A pipe is installed along the middle of the bed. Riser pipes are installed periodically to a height well above the final height of the crop. A total height of 0.6 m is sufficient for bedding plants flats and 1.8 m for fresh flowers. A nozzle is installed at the top of each riser. Nozzles vary from those that throw a 360° pattern continuously to types that rotate around a 360° circle. Trays are sometimes placed under pots to collect water that would otherwise fall on the ground between pots and is wasted. Each tray is square and meets the adjacent tray. In this way nearly all water is intercepted. Each tray has a depression to accommodate the pot and is then angled upward from the pot toward the tray perimeter. The trays also have drain holes, which allow drainage of excess water and store certain quantity, which is subsequently absorbed by the substrate.

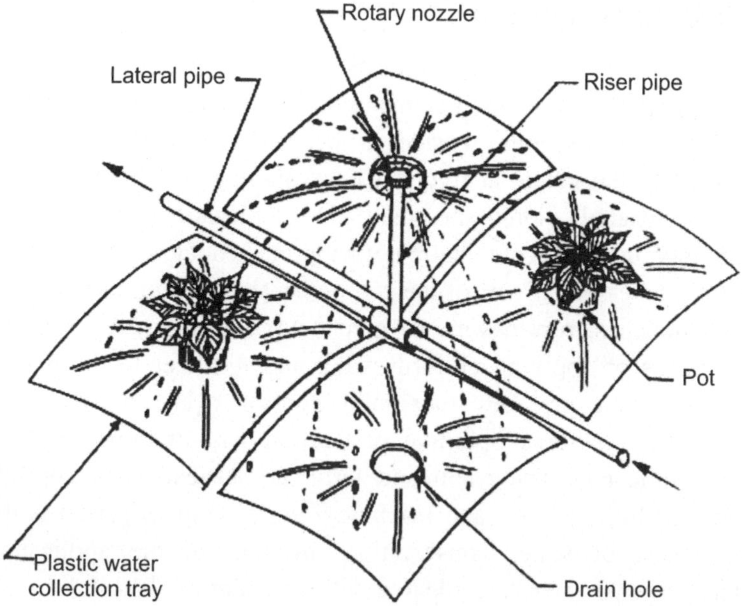

Fig. 14.2 Schematic diagram of overhead sprinkle watering system.

14.5 Boom Watering

Boom watering can function either as open or a closed system, and is used often for the production of seedlings grown in plug trays. Plug trays are plastic trays that have width and length dimensions of approximately 0.30 × 0.61 m, a depth of 13 to 38 mm, and contain about 100 to 800 cells. Each seedling grows in its own individual cell. Precision of watering is extremely important during the 2 to 8 week production time of plug seedlings. A boom watering system generally consists of a water pipe boom that extends from one side of a greenhouse bay to the other. The pipe is fitted with nozzles that can spray either water or fertilizer solution down onto the crop. The boom is attached at its center point to a carriage that rides along rails, often suspended above the center walk of the greenhouse bay. In this way, the boom can pass from one end of the bay to the other. The boom is propelled by an electrical motor. The quantity of water delivered per unit area of plants is adjusted by the speed at which the boom travels.

14.6 Drip Irrigation

Drip irrigation, often referred to as trickle irrigation, consists of laying plastic tubes of small diameter on the surface or subsurface of the field or greenhouse beside or beneath the plants. Water is delivered to the plants at frequent intervals through small holes or emitters located along the tube. Drip irrigation systems are commonly used in combination with protected agriculture, as an integral and essential part of the comprehensive design. When using plastic mulches, row covers, or greenhouses, drip irrigation is the only means of applying uniform water and fertilizer to the plants. Drip irrigation provides maximum control over environmental variability; it assures optimum production with minimal uses of water, while conserving soil and fertilizer nutrients; and controls water, fertilizer, labour, and machinery costs. Drip irrigation is the best means of water conservation. In general, the application efficiency is 90 to 95%, compared with sprinkler at 70% and furrow irrigation at 60 to 80%, depending on soil type, level of field and how water is applied to the furrows. Drip irrigation is not only recommended for protected agriculture but also for open field crop production, especially in arid and semi-arid regions of the world.

Drip irrigation is replacing surface irrigation where water is scarce or expensive, when the soil is too porous or too impervious for gravity irrigation, land leveling is impossible or very costly, water quality is poor, the climate is too windy for sprinkler irrigation, and where trained irrigation labour is not available or is expensive. In drip irrigation weed growth is reduced, since irrigation water is applied directly to the plant row and not to the entire field as with sprinkler, furrow, or flood irrigation. Placing the water in the plant row increases the fertilizer efficiency since it is injected into the irrigation water and applied directly to the root zone. Plant foliage diseases may be reduced since the foliage is not wetted during irrigation. One of the disadvantages of drip irrigation is the initial cost of equipment per acre, which may be higher than other systems of irrigation. However, these costs must be evaluated through comparison with the expense of land preparation and maintenance often required by surface irrigation.

Basic equipment for drip irrigation consists of a pump, a main line, delivery pipes, manifold, and drip tape laterals or emitters (Fig. 14.3). The head, between the pump and the pipeline network, usually consists of control valves, couplings, filters, time clocks, fertilizer injectors, pressure regulators, flow meters, and gauges. Since the water passes through very small outlets in emitters, it is an absolute necessity that it should be screened, filtered, or both, before it is distributed in the pipe system. The initial field positioning and layout of a drip system is influenced by the topography of the land and the cost of various system configurations. Design considerations should also include the relationship between the various system components and the farm equipment required to plant, cultivate, maintain and harvest the crop.

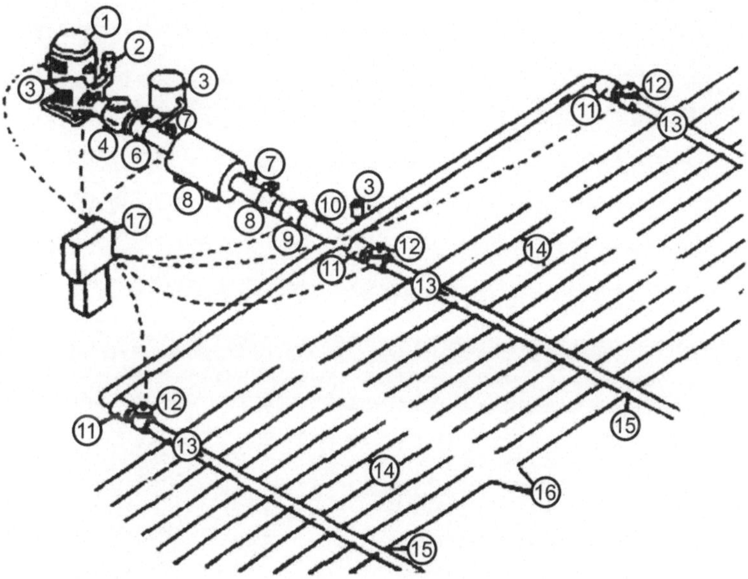

1. Pump
2. Pressure relief valve
3. Air vents (at all high points)
4. Check valve
5. Filter injector/tank
6. Mainline valve or gate
7. Pressure gauges
8. Filter
9. Mainline
10. Submain secondary filter
11. Field control valves
12. Submains
13. Drip tape laterals
14. Lateral hook up
15. Drain / flush valves
16. System controller

Fig. 14.3 A typical layout of drip irrigation system.

REVIEW QUESTIONS

1. What are the three important rules of application of irrigation water and explain?
2. Give a brief note on the methods mentioned below:
   (a) Hand watering
   (b) Boom watering
3. Write short notes with suitable sketches on the following:
   (a) Perimeter watering
   (b) Over-head sprinklers
4. Describe with a schematic layout diagram of the drip irrigation system.

Chapter 15

GREENHOUSE UTILIZATION IN OFF-SEASON

In open field agriculture, laying the field fallow in off-season replenishes it; but in greenhouse cultivation, where all growing factors are controlled, non-utilization of greenhouse in off-season is lost opportunity. The heat generated inside greenhouse can be beneficially utilized in crop processing operations like drying and curing during off-season. Drying is traditional method for preserving the food. It also helps in easy transport since the dried food becomes lighter because of moisture evaporation. Drying of seeds prevents germination and growth of fungi and bacteria. The traditional practice of drying agricultural produce in the developing countries is sun drying. In this method, the produce is spread in thin layers in open sun for drying. An alternative to the sun drying is sought, as it is seasonal, intermittent, slow and unhygienic. The moisture content and the temperature at which the food product is to be dried is always fixed. Proper maintenance of these factors is possible only in controlled mechanical drying. The energy demand of conventional mechanical dryers is met by electricity, fossil fuels, firewood and these, sources are becoming scarce. Solar energy can be an alternative source for drying of food and solar dryers are employed for the purpose. The use of the greenhouse as a dryer is the latest development. The drying capabilities of the greenhouse can also be utilised for conditioning operations such as curing tobacco leaves, while guarding the harvest from rain damage. This chapter deals with greenhouse utilization for drying of agricultural produce, curing of tobacco, the future and research needs in greenhouse technology.

15.1 Drying of Agricultural Produce

In an efficiently managed greenhouse CEA, there will not be any time gap between crops. However, for some other management reasons, if crops are not grown in a particular period, the greenhouse can be utilised as a solar dryer. A small amount of 15 to 30% of the incoming solar radiation is reflected back from the surface of the greenhouse, with the remainder is transmitted into the interior. Most of this transmitted radiation is absorbed by plants, soil and other internal surfaces, the rest being reflected. The usage of greenhouse for the purpose of the drying is of recent origin. Papadikas et al. (1981) investigated the use of greenhouse type solar dryer for drying grapes. Khollieve et al. (1982) developed a greenhouse type fruit dryer cum hot house to be used as a dryer in summer and as a hot house in winter. These researchers were successful in advocating the year round utilization of the greenhouse facility, and thus reducing the operation cost in year round basis. In general, the produce is dried in thin layers in the greenhouse. As in sun drying, the produce is spread in trays covering the greenhouse area. The trays can be fabricated with sheet metal and wire mesh. The trays should be arranged horizontally on existing growing benches or frames. For better results, proper ventilation should be provided by either forced or natural ventilation, to remove the moisture liberating from the products and to control the air temperature inside the greenhouse. The natural ventilation can be enhanced by using a black LDPE chimney connected to the greenhouse (Radha Manohar, 1993).

15.2 Curing of Tobacco

Tobacco is an important foreign exchange earning commercial crop of India, which provides employment opportunities to lakhs of people. Curing of tobacco is a delicate and vital process in producing good quality leaves. Tobacco curing essentially refers to drying of the harvested fresh tobacco leaves under controlled temperature, humidity and ventilation in order to initiate the essential bio-chemical processes. Success of curing also depends on the condition of harvested leaves and their degree of maturity. The usual curing methods are flue, air, pit, fire, and sun curing. Open field sun curing is the cheapest method of curing. The drying capabilities of greenhouse can be successfully utilised for curing the tobacco. Different stages of tobacco curing require specific environmental conditions for the best product, which can be maintained easily in a greenhouse. Following are the recommendations made by The Central Tobacco Research Institute, Rajamundry, Andhra Pradesh, India, on the environmental parameters for different stages of curing tobacco. For yellowing, the air temperature and relative humidity should be 30 to 40.5°C and 67 to 85% RH respectively. For fixing colour, the air temperature and relative humidity should be 40.5 to 48.8°C and 45 to 65% RH, respectively. Whereas for leaf drying, the air temperature and relative humidity should be 48.8 to 62.8°C and 31 to 33% RH and for stem drying 62.8 to 71.1°C and 17 to 23% RH respectively. Obviously, greenhouse also functions as rain shelter and guards the crop from rain caused damages.

The harvested tobacco leaves are made into bunches of few leaves by knots and are arranged serially on strings. Scaffoldings should be erected inside the greenhouse and the strings with leaf bunches are tied to them, for the tobacco curing process. To increase the capacity, the strings are tied with judicious gap between them and also put in tiers. As curing progresses the leaves loose the moisture and the string will become lighter and the initial sag in the strings can be corrected. For maintaining uniform product quality, the strings can be cycled among the tiers in a specified sequence. Humidity and temperature control by proper ventilation and frequent inspection is important in tobacco curing operations.

15.3 Future and Research Needs in Greenhouse Technology

In spite of the constraints in the use of protected agriculture, the future is promising. For countries not yet using any system of protected agriculture, instead of dramatic scientific breakthroughs, a series of relatively modest technological improvements are required. For greenhouse crops, research should concentrate on, among other aspects, the following:

1. Design engineering of a low cost CEA structure which is ventilated, heated, and cooled by solar and solar-effect phenomena, and other alternative energy sources.
2. Materials engineering, particularly in the development of a low cost, long lasting, selective transparent film for CEA roof structures.
3. Development of low cost night time insulation devices and techniques.
4. Design of plant bioengineering program to develop new, temperature tolerant, machine harvestable, disease resistant greenhouse cultivars.
5. Root temperature studies to determine influences on growth rates and plant development.
6. Disease control of waterborne pathogens in closed hydroponic systems by filtration and UV radiation.
7. Integrated pest management systems for greenhouse applications in order to minimize the need for pesticides.
8. The development and governmental approval of chemicals for disease and pest control in greenhouses.
9. New aggregate materials, which can substitute for European rock wool, for low cost installation and maintenance.
10. Wider utilization of industrial waste heat for greenhouse heating.

Protected agriculture is a technical reality. Such production systems are extending the growing seasons in many regions of the world and producing horticultural crops in regions, where field grown fresh vegetables and ornamentals are not available for most of the time in a year. As consumers become increasingly aware of quality differences, the demand for products of protected agriculture will increase provided they have the buying power to purchase such commodities. The economic well being of many communities throughout the world has been enhanced by the development and use of protected agriculture. Such systems offer many new alternatives and opportunities for future population, new systems that encourage conservation and preservation of the environment rather than exploitation of the land and water.

REVIEW QUESTIONS

1. What is drying of agricultural produce and give the features of sun drying?
2. What are the possible uses of greenhouse in off-season?
3. Explain the method of using greenhouse as a dryer of agricultural produce.
4. Describe the process of curing of tobacco in greenhouse.
5. List out the future research needs in greenhouse technology.

Chapter 16

SIMPLIFIED PROTECTED AGRICULTURE TECHNIQUES - PLASTIC MULCHES

The financial return for producing early crops may be high, but the risk involved is equally high. The protected agriculture techniques ensure to reduce the risks, if not eliminate them in total. Off-season crop production means more than just early spring cropping, which includes production during times of adverse climatic conditions of summer or winter. The additional cost of protected agriculture is more than compensated by the good yield of the crop. Farmers have devised many methods of protective agriculture to guard the crops against the cold and frost. These include smoke, wind machines, wetting agents, chemical fogs, bacterial spraying, sprinkling, hot caps, and brushing. Mulching in India, especially synthetic mulches, is in its initial stages; hence the requirement of the film per farmer is likely to be very small. This chapter deals with functions and requirements, types, detail of plastic mulches, mulch laying and disposal of mulches.

16.1 Functions and Requirements of Mulches

Mulching is defined as the practice of covering the soil surface around the root zone of the plant with suitable materials to create congenial conditions for the growth and development of crop. A typical arrangement of plastic mulch application for crop production has the features like mulch film laying over the crop bed, drip irrigation lines under the film, holes on the film for plant growth, and the film secured by burying its edges (Fig. 16.1). Mulching is an effective practice to restrict weed growth, reduce compaction, conserve moisture and reduce the effect of soil borne diseases through soil solarization. These factors increase crop growth and yield and promote early harvest in some cases. Synthetic mulches will continue to be used, particularly in the intensive cultivation of valuable crops.

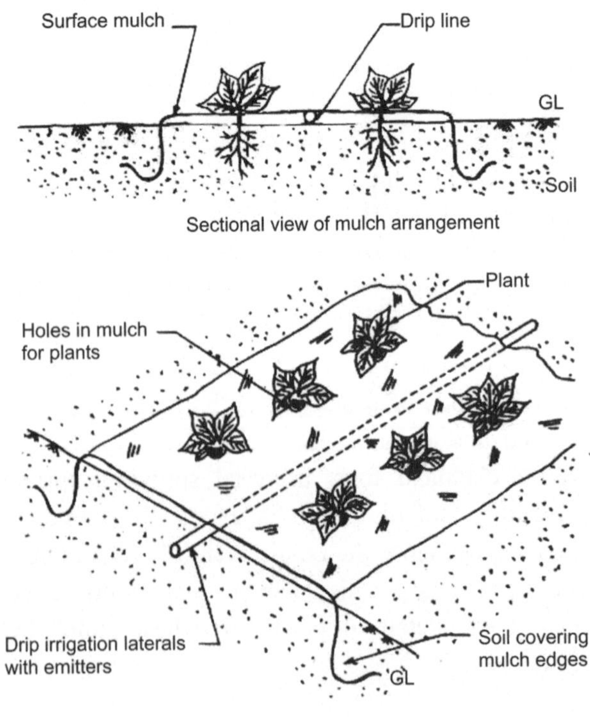

Fig. 16.1 A typical arrangement for crop mulches.

The causes that contribute to the spread of synthetic mulch culture in crop production are:

1. The water shortages in arid and semi-arid regions.
2. The need to increase production in limited space and for long duration.
3. Shortage of plant nutrients requiring more efficient fertilizer use.
4. The need for non chemical pest and weed control.
5. Sanitary regulations for fresh produce, which require the crop to be kept away from the soil surface.

As a covering material, the mulches can perform the following functions that ensure higher returns to the grower:

1. Moisture conservation in rainfed area.
2. Reduction of irrigation frequencies in irrigated areas.
3. Soil temperature moderation.
4. Weed control.
5. Soil solarization for control of soil borne diseases.
6. Better quality of produce.
7. Reducing rain impact, prevention of soil erosion and maintenance of soil structure.
8. Enhancement of overall crop production.

To achieve the above functions, the mulch material should have specific physical properties. The following are the required properties of a good mulching material:

1. It should be air proof so that no moist air escapes.
2. It should be thermal proof for prevention of heat transmission and evaporation.
3. It should be durable at least for one crop season.

4. It should have good tear or puncture strength and good capacity for light transmission.
5. It should be light in weight and easy to dispose.

16.2 Types of Mulches

Selection of mulch material has to be made based on the existing environmental condition, type of crop, durability of the mulch and cost of the mulch. The functions and applications of different types of mulch material vary with their properties. Mulches can be classified based on their sources as natural, petroleum, paper, and plastic polyethylene.

16.2.1 Natural Mulches

Natural mulches such as leaves, straw, sawdust, peat moss, and compost have been used for centuries to control weeds and to hold moisture in the soil. Straw is sometimes placed over low growing crops such as strawberries to protect against freezing. These organic materials except petroleum mulches are not been employed extensively in commercial production at present.

16.2.2 Petroleum Mulches

Petroleum mulches of organic origin, also called as liquid mulches, were popular during the early 1950s. These water emulsions of petroleum resins are formulated for spraying by adding an appropriate solvent and a suitable surfactant. This gel-like formulation sprayed over the soil surface is reported to have increased the yields by 50% on carrots, onions, lettuce, turnips, and radishes. The effective period is limited to the first few weeks after planting and it is rarely used in agriculture because of its incapacity to control the weed growth and it is very messy to apply.

16.2.3 Paper Mulches

Paper mulches came into being in the early 1920s, but are not adapted presently for commercial vegetable production due to their short life, high cost of material and labour, and unsuitability for mechanization. Later in late 1950s, improved formulations of paper including combinations of paper and polyethylene, foils and waxes were used as mulches. For many years paper was used in individual plant covers or tent-type hot caps to protect young plants, and the ear heads, or plants in the field. Although these covers helped to protect plants from the early spring frosts and winds, it was found that the brown paper used reduced the light to the plants and thereby making them more succulent and spindly in growth.

16.2.4 Plastic Polyethylene Mulches

It is only in the last fifty years that synthetic materials have altered the methods and benefits of mulching. Their potential for mulching was established by early research projects employing polyethylene, foil, and paper. Out of these mulches, only those made of plastic polyethylene are still used in the agricultural industry. If properly managed, plastic mulch can provide significant increase in yield. Plastic mulch increased yields in several crops, such as tomatoes, peppers, eggplant, muskmelons, summer squash, cucumbers, watermelons, and strawberries. It even doubled production in some cases. Plastic mulch can increase yield and improve quality of product by modifying soil temperature and controlling soil moisture. Mulch can facilitate fertilizer placement and reduce the loss of nutrients through leaching. Mulches can also provide a barrier to soil pathogens. In spite of the advantages, the high cost of synthetic mulches has limited their use in commercial production. At present synthetic mulches are used for crops of high value per unit area. The cost of mulch can be reduced if the mulches are made of thinner films, and the latest trend is in this direction.

Plastic mulch is available in sheets of various widths, colours and thicknesses. Various thicknesses of films, expressed in J.tm (microns), are used for different crops. For short duration crops (3 to 4 months), such as vegetables, strawberry, and sugar beet a 25 μm thickness is used. Medium duration crops (11 to 12 months), such as flowers, papaya, pineapple fruit crops in the initial stages require a 50 μm film. All fruit crops of long duration (more than 12 months require a 100 or 200 μm thick film. Black is the most common colour of polyethylene mulch. However, there is growing interest in the use of clear plastic since of its better light transmission which increases the soil temperature in cold climates. Thereby it promotes earlier growth and higher yield than black plastic film. The area coverage under mulch also varies from crop to crop. Judicial application of the covers based on the crop only results in proper economics. For the initial stages of orchard crops, 20% area coverage is required. Fruit crops like mango, guava, lemon, pomegranate, medium stage orchard crops, cucurbits, and melons require 40% coverage. Area coverage of 40 to 60% is needed for fruit crops like papaya and medium sized fruit trees and strawberry. Full grown fruit trees require 70 to 80%, whereas for soil solarization and crops grown inside greenhouse 100% area coverage is essential. The quantity of film required per unit area may vary with the thickness of film used and extent of area coverage, and it varies directly with these parameters.

16.3 Plastic Mulches

Of the different types of synthetic mulches, plastic mulches are the most popular type. Application of plastic mulches in the area of crop production is of recent origin, but they are widely adopted now-a-days. A variety of plastic products for mulch application are available, as in the case of flexible plastic covering materials for roof application. Plastic mulches have several advantages over mulches of other sources. Research and development activities are, at present, centered on the plastic mulches because of the advantages they offer.

16.3.1 Types of Plastic Mulches

Several types of plastic mulches are now available in the market as a result of research to achieve more desirable characteristics of the mulch materials. In the mid 1980s, infrared transmitting (IRT) mulch was introduced. IRT mulch became an intermediate product between black and clear mulch, achieving weed control as with black mulch and increasing soil temperature of clear mulch. IRT mulch absorbs most of the visible radiation, which forms the major part of PAR and supports the weed growth. Reflective mulches like aluminium foil on paper, aluminium on black polyethylene, black polyethylene and white on black polyethylene, are found to repel certain insects such as aphids. The common material used for mulch film is low density polyethylene (LDPE). But extra low density (LLDPE) and high density polyethylene (HDPE) is also used. Generally, LDPE film is 0.014 μm thick. Other films such as LLDPE, HDPE, LDPE mixed with HDPE, along with LLDPE mixed with HDPE, is only 0.008 to 0.01 μm thick. Very thin films are popular with the growers, since the growth benefits of the thin mulch are the same as that of the 0.014 μm films and the cost is 30% lesser.

Most of the mulch films are clear although silver, black, and white films are used scarcely. Herbicide films with weed killing property and photodegradable films are being studied and tested. Photodegradable plastic mulches have many attributes of standard polyethylene films. The major difference is that photodegradable mulches decompose after the film receives a certain amount of UV light. When the degradable mulch receives sufficient light it becomes brittle and develops cracks, tears, and holes. Small sections of mulch, usually less than 5 to 6 cm^2, may be torn off and blown away by the wind. The film finally disintegrates into small flakes and disappears into the soil. The edges of the mulch covered by soil, which do not receive UV radiation will retain their strength and decompose very slowly. Exposure of the covered edges to light will initiate the breakdown process and causes considerable decomposition before field preparation for the next crop. Biodegradable mulches are still in the experimental stage. When good biodegradable mulches come onto market, a great breakthrough will be made in reducing the cost of plastic removal from field and its disposal. The most promising biodegradable film formulations contain about 40% starch and 30% of polyethylene-co-acrylic acid and 30% polyethylene.

16.3.2 Advantages of Plastic Mulches

Plastic mulches provide the following advantages:

1. *Early crop*: Earlier yields are produced by accelerating the plant growth by raising the soil temperature in planting bed.

The yield advancement may vary between 7 to 21 days based on the temperature rise depending on the colour. Darker the colour lesser will be the temperature as well as the yield advancement. White or the composite white-on-black mulch creates a cooler soil temperature than either clear or black. It is preferred for certain crops.

2. *Lesser weed infestation*: The mulches which block the transmission of the PAR, such as black and white-on-black plastic reduces or eliminates the weed problems. Clear plastic was not suitable in this regard. Gray plastic mulch provides some advantage in weed control, being intermediate in transmitting the PAR. Since much of the IR radiation is absorbed at the surface of the gray film, the surface heat is sufficient to burn weeds when they touch the film. Since more heat reaches the soil through gray film, earlier harvest is obtained than with black film.

3. *Reduced evaporation:* Mulches reduce soil water loss owing to their water barrier property. The frequency of irrigation can be reduced because of the maintenance of uniform soil moisture.

4. *Reduced nutrient leaching*: Nitrogen and potassium are easily leached without plastic mulching.

5. *Reduced soil compaction:* The soil under the plastic mulches will remain loose, friable, and well aerated.

6. *Elimination of intercultural operations*: Cultivation is eliminated, except for the area between the mulch strips.

7. *Cleaner produce*: Since the produce does not come into direct contact with the soil, it is cleaner with less rot and blemishes. Such cleaner product requires less attention in grading, packing and processmg.

8. *Possibility of fumigation*: Mulches increase the effectiveness of chemicals applied as soil fumigants due to their relative air tightness.

9. *Reduced water logging*: Water is shed from the row area by the raised, tapered bed although not all plastic mulch is used only on raised beds.

10. *Pest repulsion*: Use of reflective mulch helps to repel insect vectors of virus diseases.

16.4 Technique of Mulch Laying

Proper planning and careful execution of mulch laying increase the effectiveness and reduces the maintenance. For fresh laying of mulches, the land should be prepared properly with necessary arrangements like land leveling, soil protection, drip irrigation layout and so on. Mulch should be laid in a non-windy condition. The mulch material should be held tight without any folds while laying. Borders should be anchored well inside the soil. In case of "Pre-planting-mulches", the mulch material should be punched at the required distances as per crop spacing and laid on the bed, and later the seeds or transplants should be planted in the holes. The mulch material should be cut 50 mm larger than the inter row spacing and the two adjacent sheets should be stapled in case the mulch is laid after establishment of the plants. Care should be taken so that the film is not stretched tightly. It should be loose enough to overcome the expansion and shrinkage condition caused by temperature variation and the impacts of cultural operations. The film should not be laid on the hottest time of the day.

16.5 Disposal of Mulches

The disposal of waste mulch is of great concern as large landfills become overburdened with waste plastic. Polyethylene mulch does not decompose and must be removed from the field or it will interfere with future tillage. Growers are themselves responsible for handling the wastes and, in the process, must not produce any air or water pollution. It is illegal to carelessly discard the waste plastic in a manner that may create obstacles in rivers and other public places. The following are the three methods generally employed in plastic waste disposal:

1. *Recycling*: Recycling is a method of disposal of plastics in which the used material is processed to obtain different products. This method can be subdivided into five different types 1) Generation of pellets and fluff. The collected PVC wastes are graded, cleaned off foreign matter, roughly crushed, washed with water, finely crushed and dried. The reproduction ratio of used materials is approximately 50% for PVC. The products serve as half-materials in the production of plastic tiles, mats, sandals and fillers. 2) Plastic exudation of the collected plastic wastes (PVC or polyethylene) into final products, after crushing and melting without washing. 3) Making of solid fuel blocks from the collected crushed polyethylene wastes after mixing with sawdust or rice husk. Such fuel blocks may have calorific values ranging from 23556 to 42049 kJl/kg, which are equivalent to those of coals and cokes. 4) Production of hydrophobic materials for drainage from the waste PVC through proper treatment. 5) By pyrolysis, oil or gas can be produced from the polyethylene waste.

2. *Burial*: Waste plastics that are not suitable for reproduction must be buried according to the law regulating plastic waste disposal. The place and method of burial and pre-treatment are regulated by the prevailing law. Generally wastelands having no scope for future cultivation should be selected for the purpose.

3. *Incineration:* Incineration is burning the wastes under controlled conditions. The law also regulates incineration. Since it creates air pollution, large amount is not recommended, and the amount allowed for incineration by an authorized system is again controlled by law. More detailed and thorough approaches are needed, both technically and administratively.

Research has already established the degree of improvement that various mulches make on plant productivity. Future research will probably concentrate on understanding the micro-climate provided by the different mulches, with the goal of determining how each micro-climate can be regulated to provide the optimum conditions for specific plant species. Research efforts will also be directed in the development of cost effective and crop specific specialty films with the desirable characteristics.

REVIEW QUESTIONS

1. Define mulching and describe a typical arrangement of plastic mulch with a neat sketch.
2. Supply the functions and requirements of mulches.
3. Give a brief note on the following:
   (a) Natural mulches
   (b) Petroleum mulches
   (c) Paper mulches
   (d) Plastic polyethylene mulches
4. What are the different types of plastic mulches and their features?
5. Discuss the advantages of plastic mulches.
6. Describe the techniques of laying plastic mulches.
7. Discuss the various methods of disposal of plastic mulches.
8. What are the future research needs in the area of mulches?

Chapter 17

SIMPLIFIED PROTECTED AGRICULTURE TECHNIQUES – ROW COVERS

Since the mid fifties, row covers have become an important method of protected agriculture. During 1954, vinyl film tunnels were found to advance the harvest of cucumbers by 10 days and increase the yield by 175%. In 1963, it was found that harvesting of spring crops like carrots, lettuce, cauliflower, and rhubarb was advanced by an average of two to six weeks by covering the plants with plastic tunnels for a short period in the spring, but had no effect on total yields. A row cover is a piece of clear plastic stretched over low hoops and secured along the sides of the plant row by burying the edges and ends with soil. Floating row covers are wide sheets of clear, perforated, polyethylene or non-woven porous plastic, not supported by hoops but by the plants. Row covers, or plastic tunnels, protect crops from frost and create favorable conditions for plants to achieve early production. Before the introduction of polyethylene, muslin covered wooden box frames of 0.3 m height were used. This was a costly but effective method of producing early harvest of cucumbers from 1935 to 1945. In the mid forties a method using two separate paper caps replaced the wooden box frame. The inner cover was in the form of a cap and had a height of 0.14 m and it covered the plants. The second larger tent type paper cover of 0.21 m height was installed when the plant filled the smaller cap. The paper tent cover can be opened for ventilation and it also acts as wind break. The serious drawback with the paper covers is blocking of the PAR reaching the plants. Hence more translucent materials such as vinyl or polyethylene films are substituting paper as plant covers or hot caps. Plastic row covers were initially used in Europe, US, and Japan. PVC and polyethylene films are the common row covers used presently. There are different methods of using row covers which are proven to be viable to the particular region and this chapter deals with them along with requirement of row cover polymers.

17.1 California System

In California several methods are used to form the plastic tunnels over rows of food crops. For cucumber production, two sheets of 0.90 m polyethylene films are formed into the sides of the tunnel (Fig. 17. 1). Hoops made of 9 gauge, galvanized wire, cut in 1.75 m lengths to support the two sheets of polyethylene in the formation of tunnels. The wire is bent into an oval shape (hoop) with a span of 0.375 to 0.4 m. The hoops are spaced 1.66 to 2.3 m apart. The row covers are reinforced by 25 × 250 × 700 mm wooden stakes driven into the ground below the center of the wire hoops at a spacing of 3.5 to 5 m down the plant row. The hoops, in turn, are fastened to the stakes and wire to give stability during strong winds. Soil is used to hold the bottom edges of each polyethylene sheet. A 16 gauge wire attached to the top of the stakes is the connecting fulcrum for the two plastic sheets. Ordinary spring grip cloth clips secure the two plastic sheets to the top wire. In areas of high winds, a second wire hoop is doubled over the top of the plastic at every second or third hoop. When ventilation is desired, the plastic is simply slid down one side of the tube between the wire hoops. The top hoop secures the plastic between the hoops and reduces the flapping that may loosen and damage it. A 38 μm thick clear film can be used.

For tomato production, the construction is the same except that the wooden stakes are 2 m in length, placed 1 to 1.2 m apart down the plant row. Two wires are stapled on alternate sides of each stake at a height of 0.5 to 0.55 m from the ground. Wire hoops are set at alternate stakes in forming the tunnel shape. Cloth clips are used to hold the two 1 m sheets to the two top wires. Venting is one of the most critical features in using plastic row covers. While venting the tunnels, the plastic is opened as and when needed and secured to the wire hoops and top wires with cloth clips. Clear plastic mulch is used in combination with the row covers, where weed control is economically accomplished through the use of soil fumigation.

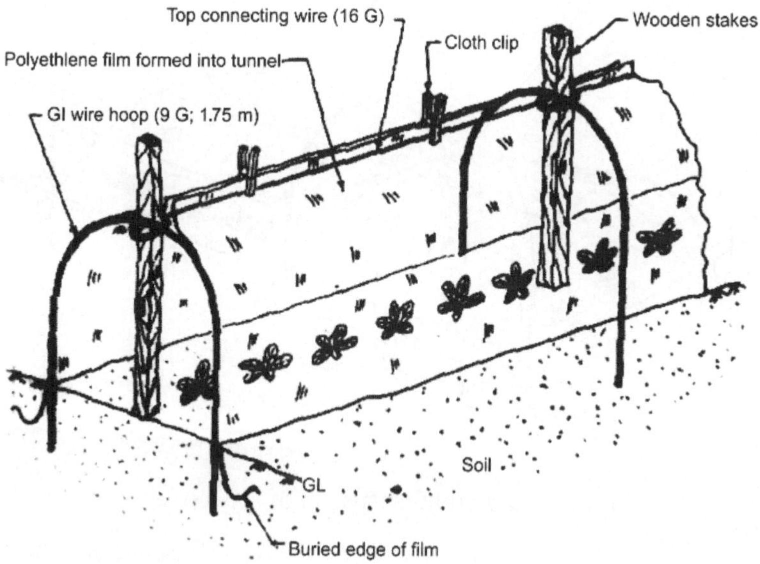

Fig. 17.1 California system of row covers.

In another row cover method, a single 1.5 m sheet of clear plastic is centered over tall stakes and forced downward. The stakes protrude out through holes on the plastic, which rides down to about the 0.5 m level from ground, where a lengthwise wire forms a tent ridge. Wire hoops often are used between the tomato stakes to form rounded tunnels, giving the plants more air space. This type of row cover is often used for rain protection. Clear plastic mulch is nearly always used in combination with the row covers. Mulch under plastic tunnel will increase the day and night temperatures of the soil, at a depth of 50 mm, by 7 to 10°C respectively.

17.2 Fernhurst System

In Fernhust system of row covers, the polyethylene sheet of 1.3 m in width and 38 μm in thickness, is spread over wire hoops that are placed at intervals of 0.6 to 0.9 m in the plant row (Fig. 17.2).

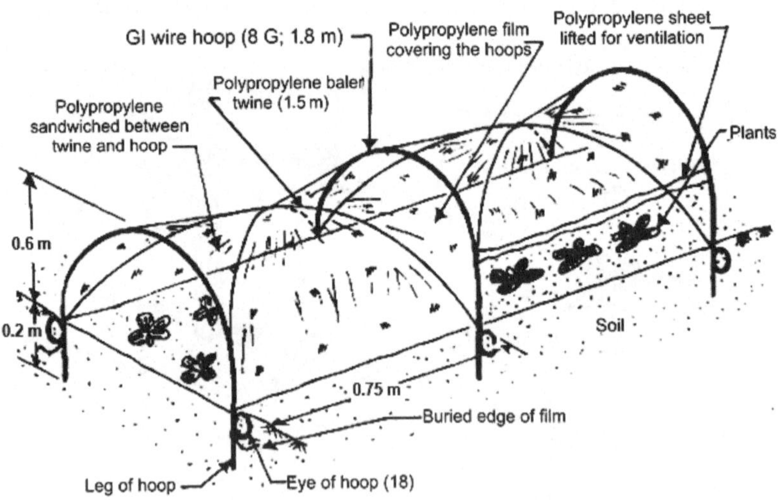

Fig. 17.2 Fernhurst system of row covers.

The hoops, 1.8 m in length are made of 8 gauge galvanized wire. Each hoop has two eyes made in the wire by a simple jig made on the farm. Each eye has a diameter of approximately 18 mm and the length of each leg is 0.2 m. Once the polyethylene is put over the hoops, the end of each row has an additional hoop for extra stability and the end of the polyethylene sheeting is buried in a trench. Lengths of polypropylene baler twine are cut 1.5 m long and loops are tied at each end. These are slipped over the eye of the hoops to hold the sheeting in place. After securing the sheeting, the eyes of the hoops are pushed into the ground so that there is no gap between the polyethylene and the soil. Ventilation of tunnels is easily achieved by lifting one edge of the film away from the soil level and pushing it towards the top of the hoop. The film moves easily between the wire and the twine, because it is securely tensioned at all times. It remains firmly in position even when the tunnels are opened.

For spraying against pests and diseases, the tunnels are opened by lifting both edges of the sheeting to the tops of the hoops. At blossom time, the tunnels are ventilated on one side by lifting an edge of the sheeting at about 0.3 m from every fifth hoop. The polypropylene twine is used instead of the additional wire that was once commonly placed over the top of the tunnels in order to secure them during wind conditions. The polypropylene twine is much cheaper in cost and does not cut or damage the polyethylene as wire does. For general guidance, the wider the tunnel the better will be the temperature conditions in the early part of the year. However, as the width of the tunnel increases, the likelihood of wind damage also increases. A low tunnel offers less wind resistance.

17.3 Perforated Plastic Tunnels

High winds remain always a problem with every method of ventilation. A technique has been developed in France whereby the plastic is perforated in order to facilitate ventilation, instead of the conventional method of opening and closing the tunnels daily (Fig. 17.3). There is only a slight difference between temperatures with the perforated and the non-perforated tunnel. But they produce similar results in early harvest and yield. From a practical point of view, the perforated plastic tunnels are less labour intensive, since solid plastic tunnels require considerable time to ensure ample ventilation in the morning and evening during an eight week period. Moreover only little condensation occurs under the perforated film. It was found that the perforated plastic sheets reduced tunnel temperatures by 5 to 6°C in comparison to unventilated solid plastic tunnels. Besides, the perforation in the plastic reduced the need for manual ventilation. Perforation can be produced by drilling the polyethylene sheet while it is still on the roll, with a low speed twist drill, aiming the drill at the center of the core. Excessively rapid drilling should be avoided as it increases the temperature, which melts and fuses the film. The perforations are approximately 6.25 mm in diameter, spaced 80 mm on the center in each direction.

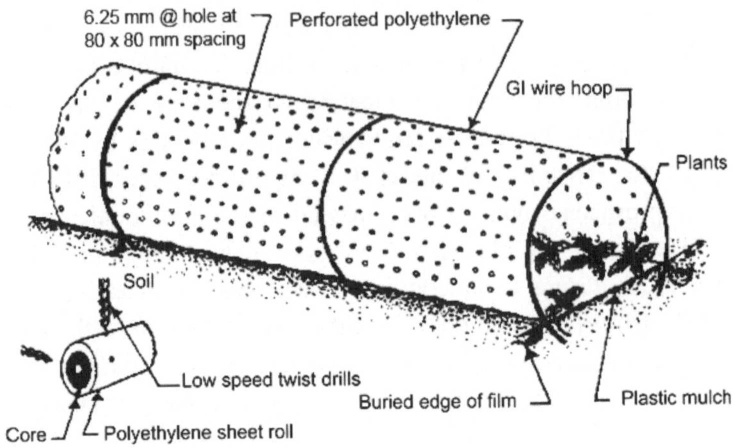

Fig. 17.3 Perforated plastic tunnels.

17.4 Slitted Row Covers

Slitted row covers have a series of crosswise slits in specific number of rows along the length, which provide ventilation on sunny days. Without these slits, plastic covers have to be manually opened and closed to provide ventilation during the day and protection from cold during night. To achieve ventilation, row covers are constructed from a single sheet of plastic, 1.5 m wide, 38 μm thick, with two rows of continuous slits, 19 mm apart and 127 mm long (Fig. 17.4). Wire hoops are buried 0.15 m deep in the soil. The procedure for installation of sheet is the same as with any row covers. Slitted row covers are generally used in combination with black polyethylene mulch. The slitted one-piece row covers show about 80% reduction in installation labour. They are self-ventilating, eliminating daily manual opening and closing of the covers and are able to withstand very gusty winds. Since the weeds are controlled by the use of black plastic mulch, the slitted row covers are free from trouble from the time of installation until the time of removal. Frost protection with the slitted covers is similar to that of the perforated polyethylene covers but is inferior to solid covers. The maximum increase in temperature inside slitted row covers is only 1.0 to 2.0°C above open field temperatures, whereas an increase of 2.5 to 4°C can be achieved with solid covers. The slitted row covers provide a reasonable compromise between maximum frost protection and a saving in labour. Crops like muskmelons, cucumbers, tomatoes, and peppers can be grown effectively under slitted row covers in combination with the black plastic mulch.

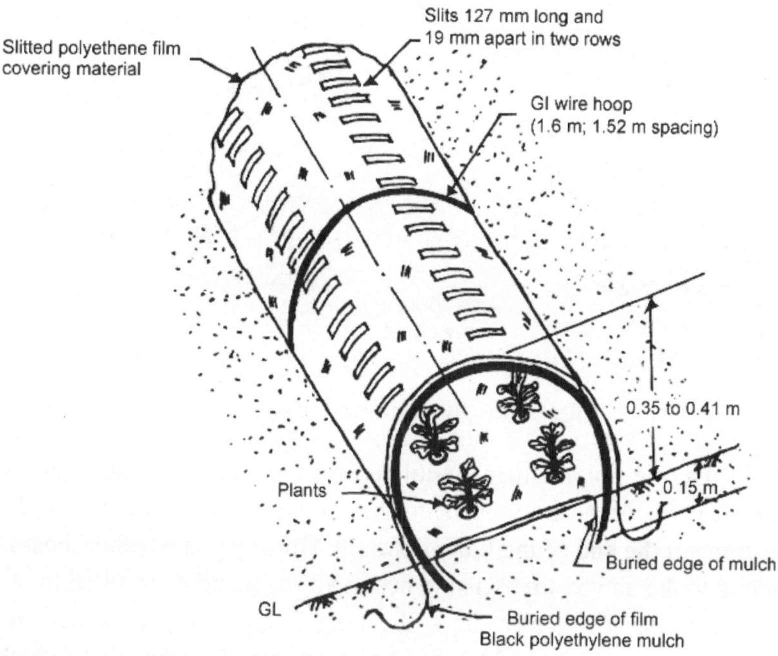

Fig. 17.4 Slitted row covers.

17.5 Air Supported Row Covers

To achieve a greater degree of frost protection to the crops, artificial heat in plastic tunnels is provided. The air supported row covers system consists of heating system, distribution chamber and air supported row cover tunnels (Fig. 17.5). The tunnels where the crops are grown, are attached continuously to the distribution chamber. Each tunnel is provided with a door at the opposite end for regulating the air flow. The fan draws the air through the air inlet and feed it to the distribution chamber, which in turn diverts the air to different tunnels. This continuous flow of diverted air will provide support to the row covers without the help of hoops. Crops such as tomatoes, cucumbers and muskmelons were grown under air supported row covers.

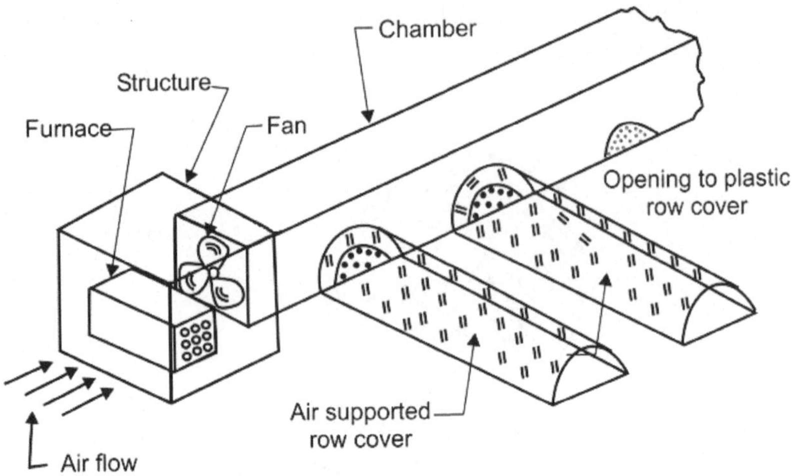

Fig. 17.5 Air supported row covers.

During hot weather, ventilation or air movement through the tunnel is increased by increasing the fan speed or by increasing the opening at the end of the tunnel or both. During cold weather, heat is added to the air stream by using heating system and distributed to the tunnels. In warm sunny days, the temperature built up inside the tunnels can be achieved by providing a smaller door opening, which in turn reduces the air movement through the tunnels. If the door opening is large, then the air movement will be more and temperature built up will be less. When the door is opened completely the temperature inside the tunnel will be approximately equal to the outside temperature.

Air temperature decreases along the length when hot air is supplied to the tunnels. In order to achieve uniform distribution of heat, a small opening is provided at the end of the tunnel. By injecting chemical dust into the fan intake, even distribution of the chemical throughout the planting can be accomplished, and pest and diseases can be controlled. If the air supported row covers are kept rigid, they can withstand the weight of the snow better than those supported by wire hoops. In these tunnels, when the heat is supplied, the harvesting of crops can be advanced up to 2 weeks. But the investment for fan and other equipment is quite high. The high expenditure is compensated by higher returns in the market. Otherwise the high expenditure in this type is not justified.

17.6 Plastic Covered Trench System

Plastic covered trench system permits early seeding, promotes early plant development, and provides frost protection. In general, there are two methods of applying polyethylene over the trenches. In the first method, polyethylene is stretched over a trench in the ground. The depth of the trench is approximately 0.18 m (Fig. 17.6). In the second method, plastic is laid across two soil ridges 0.4 m height. A mechanical mulch laying machine is used for laying the polyethylene over the trenches. Weed control is essential in such systems of protected agriculture, and is normally accomplished through the use of chemical herbicides. The polyethylene cover is removed from the trenches when the plants grow to the height of the trench. The trenches can be filled and the beds leveled by cultivation within two weeks after the removal of plastic. A plastic covered trench system is desired where low temperatures limits early growth, where the danger of frost increases the risk of early planting, and where higher prices are received for early production. Plastic covered trenches may not give the required growth response and advancement of harvest in comparison with row covers used in combination with plastic mulches. This system is far less expensive and hence is widely in use in the desert regions of the United States, Mexico, and Israel.

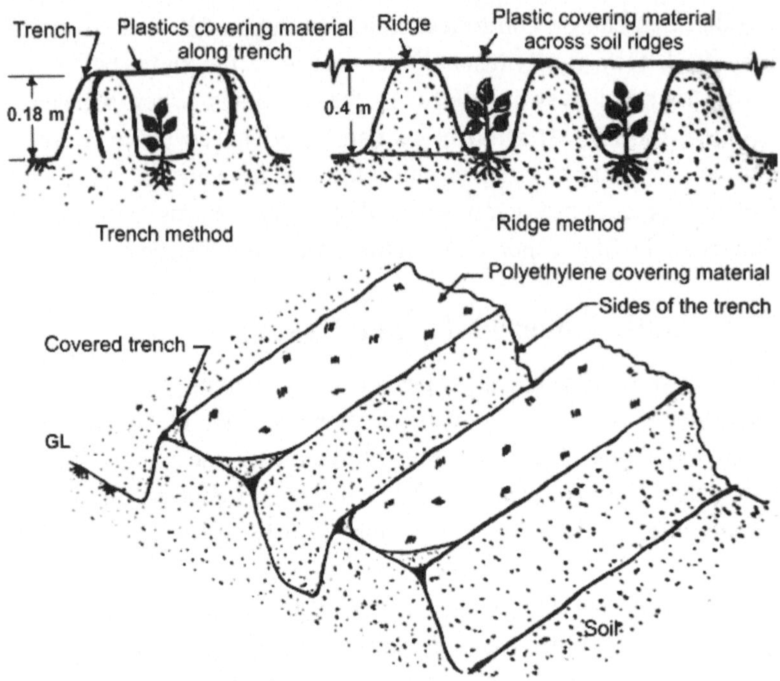

Fig. 17.6 Plastic covered trench system.

17.7 Floating Row Covers

Floating row covers can offer protection to both cool and warm season crops. The simplest form of row cover is the fabric or floating row cover, without wire or cane hoops. Floating row covers are made of spunbonded or non-woven fabrics such as polypropylene, polyamide or polyester. Polypropylene and polyester are the most commonly available fabrics. These covers are made by melting the appropriate plastic, or combination of plastics. They are sprayed as fine filaments onto a moving belt which conveys them to a bonding roller. The roller presses and fuses the filaments together.

This process is rapid and produces fabrics that are strong, light in weight, economical, and porous. Fabric can be made into very wide pieces, ranging from 1 to 10 m in width and varying lengths. The covers can be applied over a single row either by hand or by using a modified mulch applicator. Also a number of plant rows can be covered with one single large cover. When covering a single row, the cover must not be stretched tight but should be slack in the center to allow for expansion as the crop develops. For transplanted seedlings on a single row, the floating row covers can be laid after applying the plastic mulch (Fig.17.7).

Fig. 17.7 Row cover for transplanted crop.

If the single row has seeded crop then the floating row covers can be laid directly without plastic mulch application (Fig. 17.8) as the mulch may hinder the development of the seedlings. In the case of light weight covers, the edges are securely buried by putting additional weights on the soil thereby permitting safe and free flow of wind. Using a combination mechanical and manual method of applying the widest covers to a field, a team of three people can cover nearly half hectare in 40 minutes. Heavy fabrics can be reused once or more times. The light weight fabrics are seldom reused. The lightest covers, of about 10 g/m^2 are used as insect barriers. They offer protection against viruses and feeding damage from insects such as aphids, loopers, and beetles. They also prevent or discourage feeding by birds and small animals. However, these fabrics are easily damaged by livestock and other animals. They have minimal effect on temperature and light transmission.

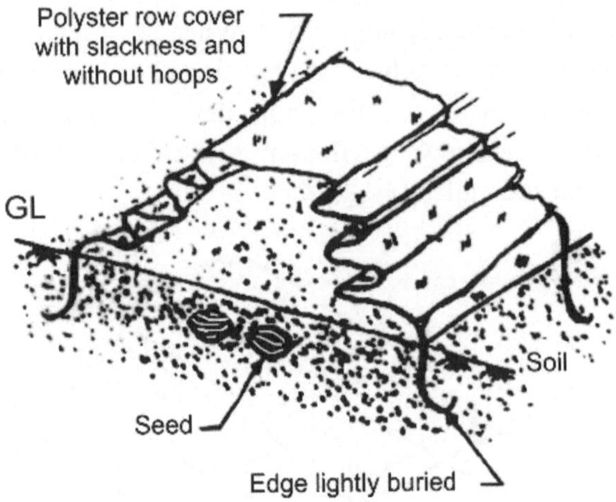

Fig. 17.8 Row cover for seeded crop.

These tunnels have the same applications as supported row tunnels or unheated greenhouses. They increase the environmental temperature by two folds or more, and protect plants from mild frosts. They help in conversion of light energy to heat energy and in trapping this heat. Although row covers are permeable to vapour, under certain conditions of temperature and humidity, moisture condenses on their inside surfaces. This condensation releases heat which increases the air temperature. The water droplets formed from the moisture on the inside of the covers act as good heat sinks. They store this heat and radiate it to the crop at night. The covers thus increase the relative humidity of the air inside and reduce water losses by transpiration or evaporation. They enhance seed germination by maintaining higher soil moisture at the surface, and prevent crusting. The covers can also modify gas concentrations around the plant. They increase CO_2 level when the decomposing organic matter is present in the soil. They modify light, thereby influencing photosynthesis, flowering and plant growth. Spunbonded field covers do the above things at a much lower cost of labour and installation than those of row runnels or plastic greenhouses. Thereby it provides flexibility to the grower who may choose to grow a protected crop for one year. The benefits from the use of floating covers are realized when row covers and field covers are integrated into one total production system. This system includes the planting schedule, proper management of the covers in regard to application, the timing of removal, the management and use of plastic mulch, irrigation and weed control under the row covers along with the other benefits of mulch.

17.8 Requirements of Row Cover Polymers

The future technology should provide row cover polymers that would change the radiation and thermal properties according to temperature. An ideal row cover should provide more insulation at low temperatures and less insulation at high temperatures in order to prevent excessive heat buildup. At present industrial polymers are used for row covers instead of polymers specially designed for agriculture use. It is important to remember that the purpose of row covers is to increase productivity by the increase of production per unit area and by reducing the crop duration. However, row covers alone will not meet this objective. They are only one segment of the overall production system. Maximum productivity and financial return will be realized only through the efficiency of the grower in crop production, management, and marketing.

REVIEW QUESTIONS

1. What is row cover and what are its similarities with greenhouse?
2. Describe California system of row covers with a neat diagram.
3. With a neat sketch describe Fernhurst system of row covers.
4. Give an account on perforated plastic tunnels with a diagram.
5. Explain with a sketch the slitted row covers.
6. What are air supported row covers, explain using a neat sketch of the complete arrangement?
7. Discuss the different methods of plastic covered trench system with suitable sketch.

8. Describe the floating row covers for transplanted and seeded crop with the help of sketches.
9. What are the requirements of ideal row cover polymers?

Chapter 18

ADVANCED PROTECTED AGRICULTURE SYSTEMS LIQUID HYDROPONICS

Antipollution regulations demand that cropping systems, which reduce the amounts of nutrients and pesticides in greenhouse effluent, should be developed. Most attention is given to closed cultural systems in which effluent with residual nutrients and pesticides, is collected, treated, and reused. Nutriculture involves the culture of plants in an inert substrate such as water (hydroponics), gravel (gravelculture), sand (sandculture), rock wool, or air (aeroponics). An inert substrate is one that neither contributes nor alters the form of plant nutrients. Inert substrates, such as rock wool or water in nutrient film technique system, afford greater control over plant nutrition than that of non-inert substrates. This chapter deals with the hydroponic system in general and nutrient film systems in particular.

18.1 Hydroponic System

Hydroponics is a technology for growing plants in nutrient solutions with or without the use of an artificial medium, such as sand, gravel, vermiculite, rock wool, peat moss and sawdust to provide mechanical support. Liquid hydroponic systems have no other supporting medium for the plant roots, whereas aggregate systems have a solid medium for support. Hydroponic systems are further categorized as open system when the nutrient solution is delivered to the plant roots and is not reused and closed system when the surplus solution is recovered, replenished, and recycled.

Hydroponic culture is possibly the most intensive method of crop production in today's agricultural industry. In combination with greenhouses or protective covers, it is highly technology oriented and capital intensive. It is also highly productive, conservative of water and land, and protective of the environment. Since regulating the aerial and root environment is a major concern in such agricultural systems, production takes place inside enclosures designed to control air and root temperatures, light, water, plant nutrition, and adverse climate. During the last 12 years, there has been increasing interest in hydroponics or soilless techniques for producing greenhouse horticultural crops. The future growth of hydroponics depends greatly on the development of production systems that are cost competitive with open field agriculture. There are many types of hydroponics systems, as well as many designs for greenhouse structures and many methods of control of the environment. Every system is not cost effective in a particular location. While the techniques of hydroponic culture in the tropics are similar to those used in temperate regions, greenhouse structures and methods of environmental control differ greatly.

Virtually all hydroponic systems in temperate regions of the world are enclosed in greenhouse type structures. The following are the functions of the general hydroponic system:

1. It should provide temperature control.
2. Reduce water loss by evaporation.
3. Reduce disease and pest infestation.
4. It should protect crops against the elements of weather, such as wind and rain.

While hydroponics and CEA are not synonymous, CEA usually accompanies hydroponics. The principal advantages of hydroponic CEA are:

1. High density.
2. Maximum crop yield.
3. Crop production where no suitable soil exists.
4. Virtual independence to ambient temperature and seasonality.
5. More efficient use of water and fertilizers.
6. Minimal use of land area.
7. Suitability for mechanization.
8. Effective disease control.

A major advantage of hydroponics, as compared to the open field agriculture (OFA), is the isolation of the crop from the underlying soil, which often has problems of disease, salinity, poor structure and drainage. The costly and time-consuming tasks of soil sterilization and cultivation are not necessary in hydroponic systems and a rapid production of crops is readily achieved. Because of the precise control over the environment and balanced supply of plant nutrients, the maximum potential yield is assured in hydroponic culture. Studies have shown that the yield of tomatoes in hydroponic CEA (Fig. 18.1) is 375 million tonnes/ha/year when compared to 100 million tonnes/ha/year in OFA.

The principal disadvantages of hydroponics relative to conventional OFA are the high costs of capital and energy inputs, and the high degree of management skills required for successful production. Capital costs may be especially excessive if the structures are artificially heated and evaporatively cooled by fan and pad systems, and have systems of environmental control that are not always needed in the tropics. Workers must be highly competent in plant science and engineering skills. Because of its higher costs, successful application of hydroponic technology is limited to crops of high economic value, to specific regions and often confined to specific seasons of the year, when OFA is not feasible. Because capital costs are much higher for CEA than for OFA, it is economical to grow only a few food crops, where field crops are totally inappropriate. Studies of prices have shown that only high quality, garden type vegetables, such as tomatoes, cucumbers, and specialty lettuce can provide break even or better revenues in hydroponic systems. Besides these vegetables, eggplant, peppers, melons, strawberries and herbs are grown commercially under hydroponic systems in Europe and Japan.

Fig. 18.1 Tomato production using nutrient film technique.

18.2 Nutrient Film Technique

Nutrient film technique (NFT) is a form of hydroponics in which plants are grown in narrow, sloped channels. A thin film of recirculating nutrient solution flows through the roots in the channels. The walls of the channels are flexible, which permit the solution to flow around the base of each plant prohibiting light and preventing evaporation. Nutrient solution is pumped to the higher end of each channel and flows past the plant roots by gravity to catchment pipes and a sump (Fig. 18.2). The solution is monitored for replenishment of nutrient salts and water before it is recycled. Capillary material in the channel prevents young plants from drying out, and the roots soon grow into a tangled mat.

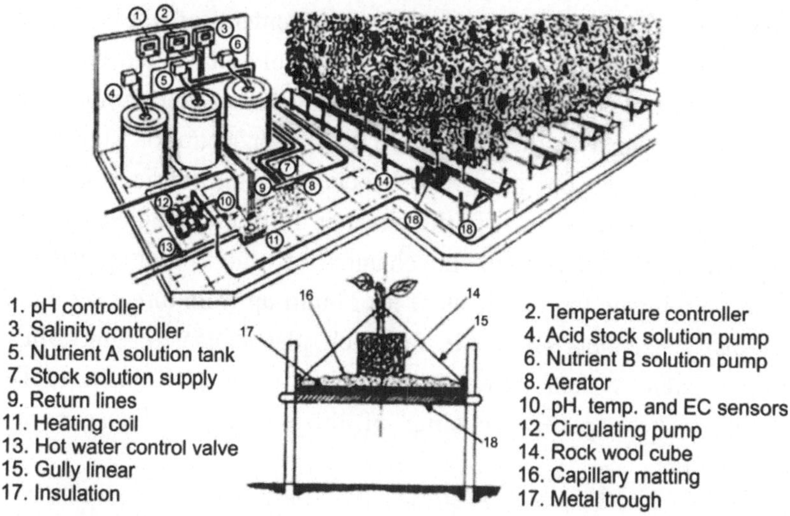

Fig. 18.2 Typical features of NFT hydroponic system.

A principal advantage of the NFT system in comparison with others is that it requires very less nutrient solution. It is therefore easier to heat the solution during winter months, to obtain optimum temperatures for root growth, and to cool it during hot summers in arid or tropical regions, thereby avoiding the bolting (formation of seed stalk) of lettuce and other undesirable plant responses. If it is necessary to treat the nutrient solution for disease control, small volumes are easier to work with.

The channels should not be greater than 15 to 20 m in length. In a level greenhouse, as the recommended slope of the channel is 1 in 50 to 1 in 75, long channels can restrict the height available for plant growth. If the length of greenhouse is more, then with the given slope the elevation difference between the ends of the channels will be so high that the plants at higher elevation will have less head space to grow. If the channel slope is less, it may result in poor aeration of solution. To assure good aeration, the nutrient solution could be introduced into channels at two or three points along the length. The flow of nutrient solution into each channel should be

2 to 3 lpm, depending on the oxygen content of the solution. The maximum temperature of the nutrient solution should be 30°C. Temperature above 30°C will adversely affect the amount of dissolved oxygen in the solution. The O_2 concentration should be approximately 5 ppm or more, especially in the nutrient solution flowing over the root mat in the channel. In tropical regions, where high temperature is common the channels of white colour are used in order to mitigate the problems of heat build-up from direct sunlight. Normally channels are made of black plastic coated with white colour. NFT system permits economical cooling of plant roots, avoiding the expensive cooling of the entire greenhouse aerial temperature.

Aeration is not a problem with NFT, as in the classical hydroponic systems, because the nutrient solution is confined to a depth of 3 mm. Most greenhouses are heated with hot water, and the method is inappropriate for pasteurization. Thus methyl bromide method of pasteurization is popular. In the sandy soils methyl bromide readily permeates into the soil as well as the plastic wall of water pipes lying within these soils. Contamination of drinking water prompted a restriction in the dosage rate of methyl bromide and threatened its future use. Disease problems can be avoided in open cultural systems, in which nutrient solution makes a single pass by the roots and then on to the drain, while still accommodating the possibility of automation. Sterile rock wool can also be used as a rooting medium in NFT. Presently, nearly all greenhouse cucumber and tomato plants in Denmark are produced in rock wool.

18.2.1 Cast Concrete Modified NFT

Covering the greenhouse floor with cast concrete shaped into NFT channels is one type of modified NFT system. Capital investment in this method is high, but maintenance is less compared with a conventional system. In a typical installation for year-round lettuce production, the concrete was cast into parallel channels of 100 mm wide, 25 mm deep, and 45 m long, on a slope of 1 to 50. The surface of the concrete was painted with epoxy resin to isolate it from the nutrient solution.

18.2.2 Movable Channels NFT

Movable benches covered with corrugated sheets are used in this system. Plants are set in the corrugations, through which nutrient solution flows. Plants are kept at close intervals when young, and spread out as more growing space is needed when they grow. The channels can be spread apart since they are arranged on movable bench tops in response to plant growth and size (Fig. 18.3). Benches are movable to allow access to growing areas. The bench tops are supported on pipe rollers and allowed to move sideways 0.7 to 1 m, providing the width needed for a working aisle. This variable plant spacing technique maximizes space utilization and leaf interception of radiation.

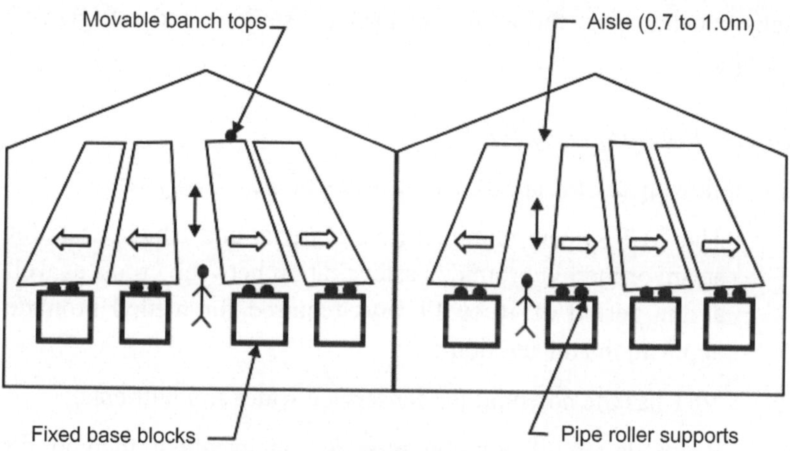

Fig. 18.3 Movable benches of modified NFT system.

The growing system without intermediate pathways between every bench would increase plant density by approximately by 25%. Flat sheets of expanded polystyrene that can be transported on movable benches have been used for lettuce production.

18.2.3 Pipe Systems

Seedlings are planted in sloping plastic tubes, having 30 mm diameter are laid in a grade of 1 in 30, arranged in horizontal tiers resembling A-frames in end-view. An A-frame system provides for high-density lettuce production. This system effectively doubles the usable growing surface and accommodates a plant density of $40/m^2$.

18.2.4 Moving Belts

This system is used for lettuce production. In this system, movable belts in NFT troughs are arranged in two tiers in which seedlings are transplanted. The upper tiers or troughs obviously shade out plants on the lower tiers, causing some reduction in the yield and quality of the latter. This effect can be reduced by eliminating some of the upper tiers to permit more radiation to enter to the lower tiers. In this system the produce can be mechanically harvested and the conveyor belts can transport the lettuce to packing stations and refrigerated storage.

18.2.5 Advantages of NFT

The following are the specific advantages of the NFT systems:

1. The NFT system eliminates the material and labour costs for steam or methyl bromide pasteurization between crops, as well as the period of 10 to 14 days required for methyl bromide application and aeration.
2. NFT has the potential for conserving water and nutrients.
3. Recirculation of solution provides an excellent method for reducing nutrient and pesticide effluent from greenhouses.
4. NFT systems have the potential for automation.
5. Formulation, testing, and adjustment of nutrient solutions can be handled at a central point, and even these operations can be automated.
6. The nutrient solutions are mechanically delivered to the crop.

7. It is possible to alter the heat level of the nutrient solution by heating or cooling to suit to the plant requirement.
8. Use of heavy root substrates and their handling is eliminated.

18.3 NFT System Cultural Procedures

Water tight channels, though do not require a lining they need a covering. This covering may be a solid material or a film plastic. Channel coverings serve to prevent water loss through evaporation, restrict light entry to prevent algal growth that will remove nutrients and plug the system, and help in controlling root temperature. The outer surface of the covering should be white or silver to reduce heat absorption and to reflect light to the plants for better growth. Air inside a black channel would become hot enough to bum roots on warm, bright days. White plastic does not sufficiently restrict light. Therefore, film plastic is sold with one (inner) surface black and the other surface white. For regions of extreme temperatures, an insulated channel covering may be constructed by using two film plastic coverings with a dead-air space between them.

In NFT, the nutrient solution is handled in a closed recirculating system (Fig. 18.4). A tank, usually built into the floor, collects solution by gravity flow from the ends of the channels. Solution is pumped from the tank to a header pipe that runs perpendicular to the upper ends of the channels. Small tubes running from the header pipe supply each channel. The flow rate should be sufficient to maintain nutrient film thickness of not more than 3 mm over the entire bottom surface of the channel. Greater depth will exclude oxygen from the roots. A flow rate of about 2 lpm per channel is required. In some systems the solution is constantly recirculated. Water should be added continuously to the head tank, as considerable volume of water will be lost through transpiration. This can be automatically done by installing a float valve on a water inlet line in the tank. The ideal nutrient concentrations for NFT culture suggested by Cooper (1979) are listed in Table 18.1.

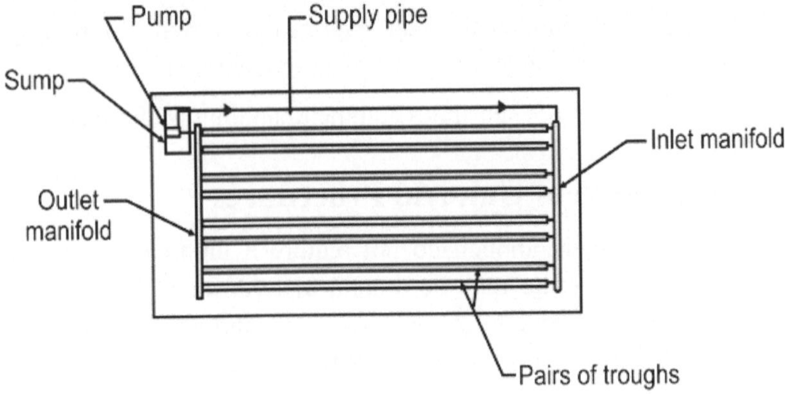

Floor plan of the total nutrient film technique system

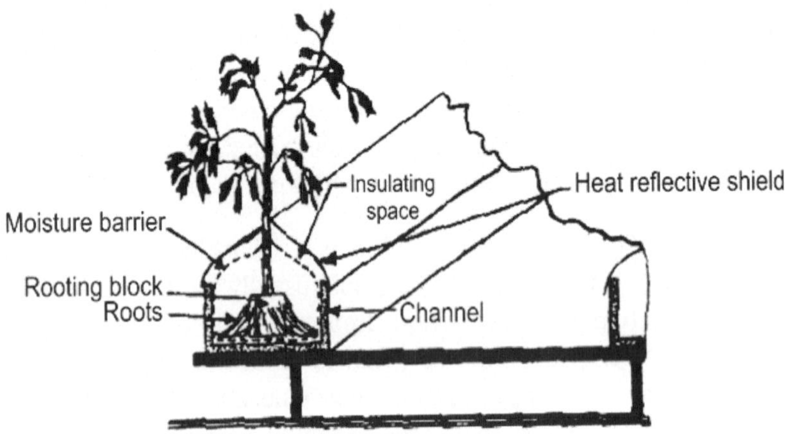

Cross-sectional view of a trough

Fig. 18.4 Simpilifed NFT system.

Sources of nutrients and required weights are presented in Table 18.2. There is no need for a firm to formulate its own nutrient solution as various companies sell NFT fertilizers. Generally, they come in two or three packages that must be added separately to the tank to prevent precipitation. It is necessary to test the pH and electrical conductivity (EC) levels (soluble salt) of the solution daily.

Table 18.1 Theoretically Ideal Concentration of Elements in Nutrient Solution for NFT Cropping

Element	Symbol	Concentration (ppm)
Nitrogen	N	200.0
Phosphorus	P	60.0
Potassium	K	300.0
Calcium	Ca	170.0
Magnesium	Mg	50.0
Iron	Fe	12.0
Manganese	Mn	2.0
Boron	B	0.3
Copper	Cu	0.1
Molybdenum	Mo	0.2
Zinc	Zn	0.1

Source: Cooper (1979)

Table 18.2 Weights of Chemical Compounds Required to give Theoretically Ideal NFT Cropping Concentration in Water.

Chemical	Formula	Weight (g/1000 l)
Potassium dihydrogen phosphate	KH_2PO_4	263.00
Potassium nitrate	KNO_3	583.00
Calcium nitrate	$Ca(NO_3)_2 4H_2O$	1003.00
Magnesium sulfate	$MgSO_4 7H_2O$	513.00
EDTA iron	$[CH_2N(CH_2COO)_2]_2FeNa$	79.00
Manganous sulfate	$MnSO_4H_2O$	6.10
Boric acid	H_2BO_3	1.70
Copper sulfate	$CuSO_4 5H_2O$	0.39
Ammonium molybdate	$(NH_4)_6MO_7O_{24}4H_2O$	0.37
Zinc sulfate	$ZNSO_4 7H_2O$	0.44

Source: Cooper (1979)

The pH level should remain in the range of 5.8 to 6.5. When pH decreases, the base, potassium hydroxide can be added. When pH increases, the acid, sulfuric acid can be added to restore the desired level.

Computerized equipment that will automatically sample nutrient solution from the holding tank, analyze it for pH, EC and individual nutrients, and make the appropriate additions of acid, base, or fertilizer is available. This equipment includes tanks of acid, base, and individual fertilizer salts, such as potassium nitrate and magnesium sulfate in concentrated form. The test results are processed in the computer to determine which nutrient salts is required and how much of each will be injected into the NFT solution. These concentrates are then automatically added. The automated system also allows the pH and nutrient concentrations of the solution to be maintained more precisely than by merely analyzing the solutions once in day. Plants to be set in an NFT system are propagated in containers such as blocks of rock wool, foam cubes, or in netlike pots containing soilless substrate. It is important that the propagation unit does not contribute peat moss or other loose substances that will plug the system. Young plants are often grown in channels in the propagation area; however, plants within the channels as well as the channels themselves are placed much closer together than they are in the final stages.

18.4 Deep Flow Hydroponics

Deep flow hydroponics is a method of growing a number of heads of lettuce or other leafy vegetables on a floating raft of expanded plastic (Fig. 18.5). One of the production systems consists of horizontal, rectangular shaped tanks lined with plastic of size, 4 × 70 m, and 0.3 m deep. The nutrient solution is monitored, replenished, recirculated, and aerated. Rectangular tanks have two distinct advantages. The nutrient pool acts as frictionless conveyor belts for planting and harvesting movable floats, and the plants are spread in a single horizontal plane for maximum interception of sunlight. Two to three-week-old seedlings are transplanted, into holes in the 25 mm thick polystyrene floats, in staggered rows with approximately 0.3 m spacing. As a crop of several floats is harvested from one end of a raceway, new floats with transplants are introduced at the other end. Long lines of floats with growing lettuce can be moved easily by simple hand pushing. Deep flow hydroponics for lettuce production is technically sound but uneconomical in the subtropics, because lettuce can be grown year round in the open field at less cost per unit produce. Such a system is better suited to tropical regions, where local open field production does not occur during the warmer months. In these areas, such production systems, in combination with root cooling, will give better yields.

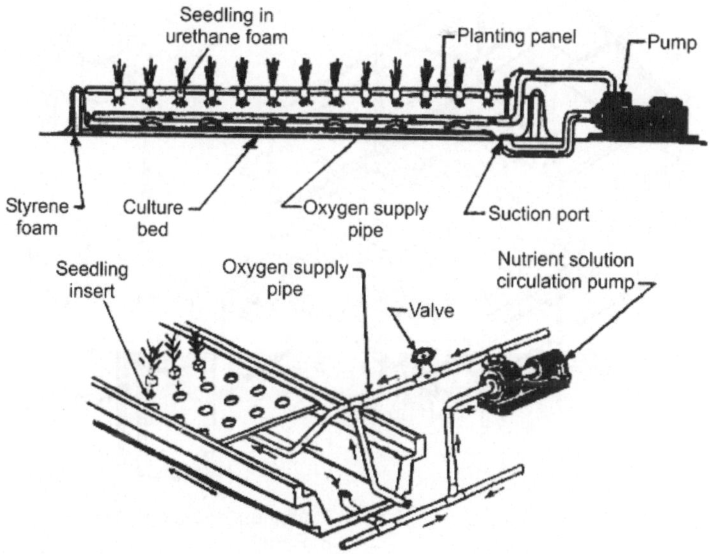

Fig. 18.5 System layout of a floating hydroponic system.

18.5 Dynamic Root Floating Hydroponic System

The dynamic root floating (DRF) system of hydroponics is similar to the deep flow hydroponic system but is designed specifically for hot and tropical regions. The major difference is the air space provided between the polystyrene growboard and the level of nutrient solution maintained in the gutter of the culture bed (Fig. 18.6). Small, fluffy feeder roots, which develop in the air space, are able to absorb much of the plant's necessary oxygen requirements, when compared to the roots in the nutrient solution which is often low in dissolved oxygen. Once the temperature of the solution rises above of 25 to 30°C, it becomes increasingly difficult to maintain the necessary dissolved oxygen in the solution. At these temperatures, the method of providing optimum oxygen levels to the plant by DRF, may be more economical than chilling the nutrient solutions to temperatures below 25°C.

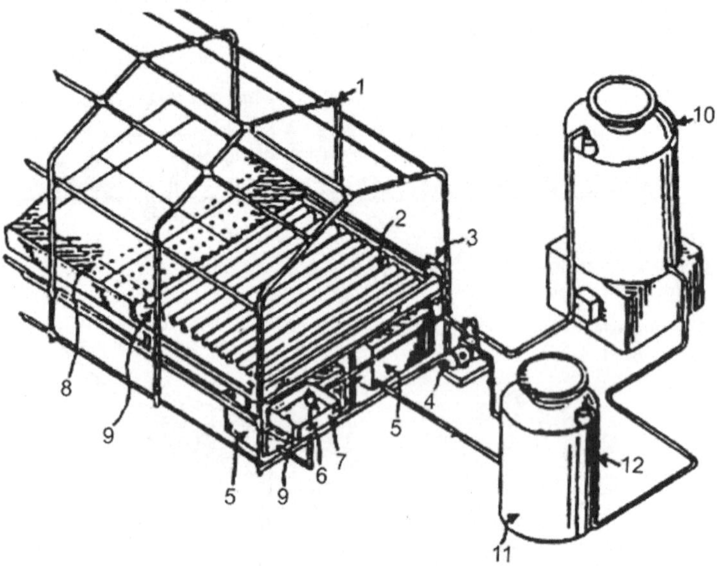

1. Pipe house
2. Culture bed
3. Aspirator
4. Pump
5. Reservoir
6. Nutrient level adjuster
7. Nutrient exchange box
8. Panel
9. Nutrient outlet plug
10. Upper nutrient tank
11. Lower nutrient tank
12. Floating switch

Fig. 18.6 Dynamic root floating hydroponic system.

In Taiwan, the DRF method has been coupled with a low-cost growing structure. This system of protected agriculture is recommended for growing regions that experience a high number of typhoons, heavy rainfall, high temperatures, and high insect populations. The DRF hydroponic system was designed to include a gutter shaped culture bed, an aspirator, nutrient level adjuster, nutrient exchange box and nutrient concentration controller plus a typhoon-proof low height plastic film greenhouse.

The framework of the typhoon-proof low height plastic greenhouse is made of galvanized iron pipe. The standard size- of the plastic house is 7.2 m long, 2.1 m wide and 1.8 m in height. The length of the structure may be enlarged depending on the market demand of the produce grown. In Taiwan, the roof of the greenhouse is covered with dew-resistant transparent PVC plastic film to prevent rain water from coming in contact with the horticultural crop. On the sides of the house, a white polyethylene plastic net prevents entry of insects. When greenhouse temperatures reach 30°C, a black polyethylene net providing 40% shade, is installed 0.1 m above the plastic house. In this method horticultural crops grown are most often free from chemical residue, since few chemical pesticides are used.

18.6 Aeroponics

It is also possible for a closed system hydroponics, where plants are grown in holes on panels of expanded polystyrene or other material and such a method is known as aeroponics. The plant roots are suspended in midair beneath the panel and are enclosed in spraying box (Fig. 18.7). The box is sealed so that the roots are in darkness, which inhibits algal growth in the prevailing saturation humidity. A misting system sprays the nutrient solution over the roots periodically. The system is normally turned on for only a few seconds every two to three minutes. This is sufficient to keep roots moist and nutrient solution aerated. The A-frame aeroponic system developed in Arizona for low, leafy crops may be feasible for commercial food production. Inside a CEA structure, these frames are oriented with the inclined slope facing east-west.

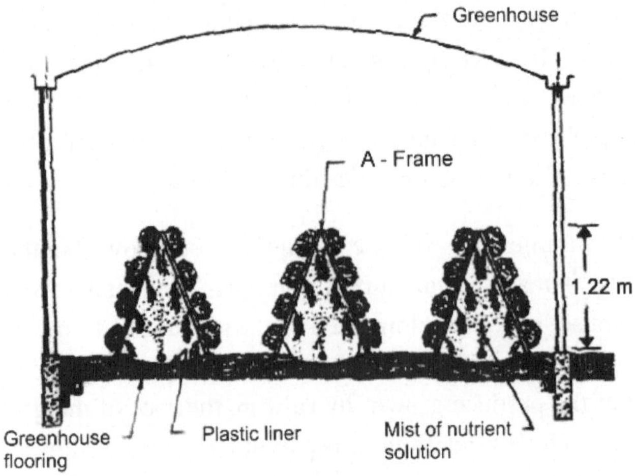

Fig. 18.7 Aeroponic system using A-frame units.

The expanded plastic panels are of standard size (1.2 × 2.4 m), mounted lengthwise, and spread 1.2 m at the base to form an equilateral triangle on the end view. The A-frame rests on the top of a panel-sized water-tight box, 0.25 m deep, which contains the nutrient solution and misting equipment. Young seedlings in small cubes of growing medium are inserted into holes in the panels, which are spaced at intervals of 0.18 m center to center. An apparent disadvantage of such a system is uneven growth resulting from variations in light intensity on the crops growing on the inclined panels. An advantage of this technique for CEA lettuce or spinach production is that twice as many plants can be accommodated per unit of floor area than in other systems, such as growing of vine crops in the greenhouse, where the cubic volume is better utilized.

REVIEW QUESTIONS

1. Define hydroponics and what are the broad categories of hydroponic system?
2. What are the basic features of hydroponic systems?
3. Describe nutrient film technique with the help of diagram showing the typical features of the system.

4. Write short notes on:
   (a) Cast concrete modified NFT system
   (b) Modified channels NFT system
   (c) Pipe NFT system
   (d) Moving belt NFT system
5. List the advantages of NFT systems.
6. Give a brief note on the cultural procedures of NFT systems.
7. Explain with a diagram the simplified NFT system.
8. Write about deep flow hydroponic system with a suitable sketch.
9. What are the features of dynamic root floating hydroponic systems?
10. Describe the aeroponic system using a neat diagram.

Chapter 19

ADVANCED PROTECTED AGRICULTURE SYSTEMS – AGGREGATE HYDROPONICS

The need to reduce production costs to meet intense international competition and the present antipollution legislation regarding nutrients and pesticides in greenhouse effluent water are resulting in the development of several alternative crop production systems for greenhouses. Aggregate hydroponics crop production systems provide both the mechanical support for the plants and the nutrient supply through inert solid mediums. As in liquid systems, the nutrient solution is delivered directly to the plant roots. Aggregate systems may be either open or closed, depending on whether surplus amounts of the solution are to be recovered or reused. Open systems do not cycle the nutrient solution, whereas in the closed systems nutrient solutions are recycled with proper replenishment. Whole-firm recirculation is a closed production system for all greenhouse crops, where the effluent from the system is reused after treatment. The various methods of open and closed systems of aggregate hydroponics and whole-firm recirculation are discussed in this chapter.

19.1 Open Systems

In most open hydroponic systems, excess nutrient solution is recovered. However, the surplus is not recycled to the plants, but is disposed off in evaporation ponds or used to irrigate adjacent landscape plantings or windbreaks. As the nutrient solution is not recycled, such open systems are less sensitive to the composition of the medium used or to the salinity of the water. These factors have prompted to conduct research with a wide range of growing media and the development of more cost-efficient designs. In addition to wide growing beds in which a sand medium is spread across the entire greenhouse floor, open systems may use troughs, trenches, bags, and slabs of porous horticultural grade rock wool. Fertilizers may be fed into the proportioners (Fig. 19.1) or may be mixed with the irrigation water in a large tank or sump (Fig. 19.2).

Automatic irrigation control manages the irrigation, which is usually programmed through a time clock. In larger installations, solenoid valves are used to irrigate only one section of a greenhouse at a time. Such system permits the use of smaller sized mechanical system.

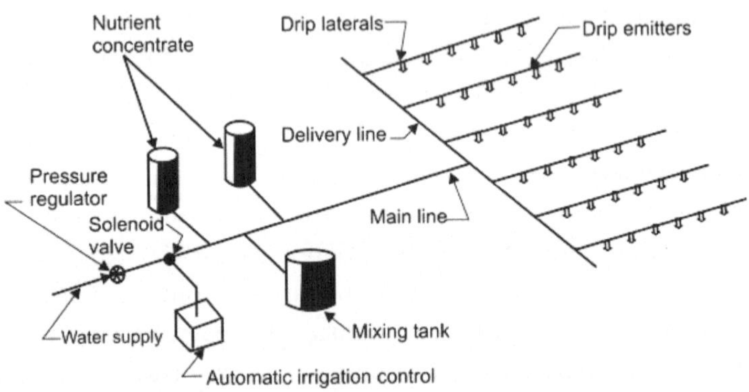

Fig. 19.1 Fertilizer proportioner method.

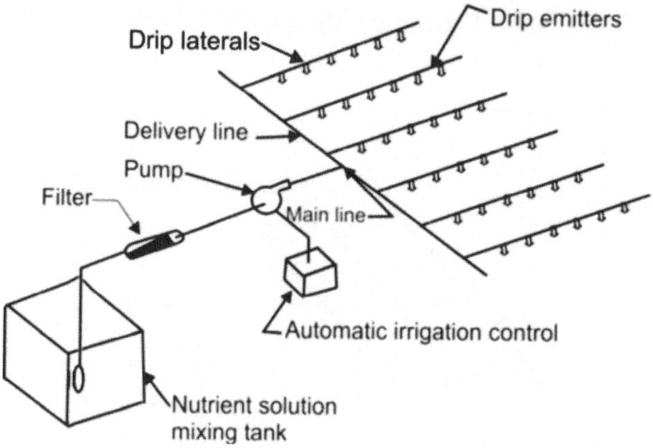

Fig. 19.2 Fertilizer mixing tank method.

19.1.1 Trough and Trench Culture

Some open aggregate systems involve relatively narrow growing beds, either as overground troughs (Fig 19.3) or subgrade trenches, whichever are more economical to construct at a given site. In both cases, the beds of growing media are separated from the rest of the greenhouse floor and confined within waterproof materials. For ease of description, this system will be referred to as trough culture. Concrete has been traditionally used for construction of permanent trough installations. Fiberglass, or plywood board covered with fiberglass, is also used. Polyethylene film, at least 0.1 mm thick is now commonly used to reduce costs. Bed depth varies with the type of growing media and about 0.25 m is a typical minimum. Length of the bed is limited only by the capability of the irrigation system, which must deliver uniform amounts of nutrient solution to each plant. Bed length should also take care of the requirements for lateral walkways for work access. A typical bed length is about 35 m. The slope should have a drop of at least 0.15 m per 35 m for good drainage and there should be a well-perforated drain pipe of agriculturally acceptable material at the bottom of the trough, beneath the growing medium. Since open systems are less sensitive than closed systems to the type of growing medium used, there has been much regional ingenuity in locating low cost inert materials for trough culture. Typical growing media include sand, vermiculite, sawdust, perlite, peat moss, mixtures of peat and vermiculite, and sand with peat or vermiculite.

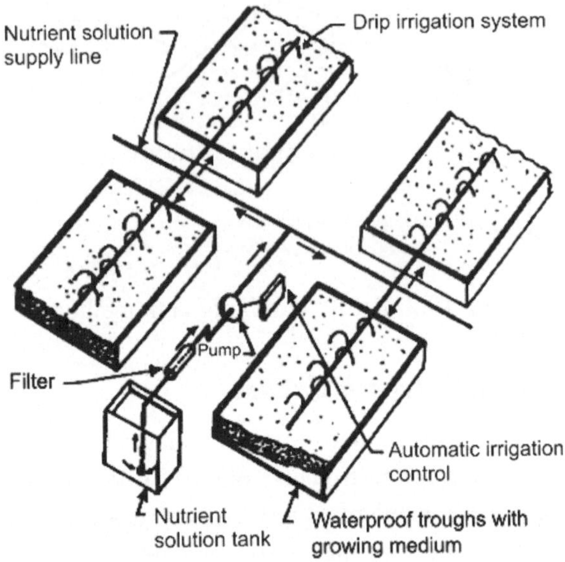

Fig. 19.3 Over ground trough culture in open aggregate hydroponics.

19.1.2 Bag Culture

Bag culture is similar to trough culture, except that the growing medium is placed in plastic bags. These bags are placed in lines on the greenhouse floor, thus avoiding the costs of troughs or trenches and of complex drainage systems. The bags can be used for at least two years and are much easier and less costly to steam sterilize than bare soil.

The bags are typically made of UV resistant polyethylene with a black interior and will last in a CEA environment for two years. The exterior of the bag should be white in deserts and other regions of high light levels; this will reflect radiation and inhibit heating of the growing medium. Conversely, a dark exterior colour is preferable in northern, low-light latitudes to absorb winter heat. Bags used for horizontal applications are usually 50 to 70 litres in capacity. Growing media for bag culture include peat, vermiculite, or a combination of both, to which polystyrene beads, small waste pieces of polystyrene, or perlite are added to reduce the total cost. When placed horizontally, bags are sealed at both ends after being filled with the medium. It is advantageous to cover the entire floor with white polyethylene film before placing the bags.

Paired rows of bags are usually placed flat, 1.5 m apart from center to center with some separation between bags, while each row is arranged end to end. This is the normal row spacing for vegetables. Holes are made in the upper surface of each bag for the introduction of seedlings, and two small slits are made at the bottom for drainage or leaching. Some moisture is introduced into each bag before planting. Supply of nutrient mix through drip irrigation, with a capillary tube leading from the main supply line to each plant, is recommended. Plants growing in high-light, high-temperature conditions will require up to 2 litres of nutrient solution per day. Moisture near the bottom of the bagged medium should be examined often. The most commonly grown crops in bag culture are tomatoes and cucumbers, as well as cut flowers. The use of bag culture is greatly dependent on the availability and cost of growing media.

19.1.3 Rock Wool Culture

Rock wool culture was pioneered in Denmark during the late 1950s. By the early 1970s, horticultural rock wool was in production in Denmark. Rock wool is produced by burning a mixture of coke, basalt, limestone and slag from iron production. At a 1600°C temperature in the furnace, the rock minerals melt. This liquid is collected from the base of the furnace. A stream of this molten rock flows onto a high-speed rotor. Droplets thrown from the rotor lengthen into fibers. The fibers are sprayed with a binding agent in an air stream, which cools and carries them to a conveyor, where they are deposited onto a belt. The pad of fibers, is then compressed between rollers to a specified density. Finally, it is cut into desired dimensions. Horticultural-grade rock wool is formulated to a prescribed higher density to provide the air and water holding requirements of plants. Rock wool used in cubes for propagation and in slabs for final stages of crops. Unlike industrial rock wool, horticultural-grade rock wool is treated with surfactants to improve water absorbance. It contains about 3% solid and 97% pore space. Rock wool is not biodegradable, but it does slowly weather. Slabs are often used for two years of cropping before disposal.

Horticultural rock wool is becoming increasingly popular as a growing medium in open hydroponic systems. Rock wool systems now receive more research attention than any other type in Europe. Cucumbers and tomatoes are the principal crops grown in rock wool. In case of soil culture steam, natural gas and methyl bromide are used as a soil fumigant for sterilization. Rock wool as a growing medium, is relatively inexpensive, inert and biologically nondegradable. It absorbs water easily, has approximately 96% pores or interstitial air spaces, the pores are evenly sized, lends itself to simplified and low cost drainage systems, and is easy to bottom heat during winter. Its versatility is such that rock wool is used in plant propagation and potting mixtures, as well as in hydroponics (Fig. 19.4). Rock wool has several inherent advantages as an aggregate:

1. It is light in weight when dry.
2. Easy to handle.
3. Simple to bottom heat.
4. Easy to steam sterilize when compared to many other types of aggregate materials.

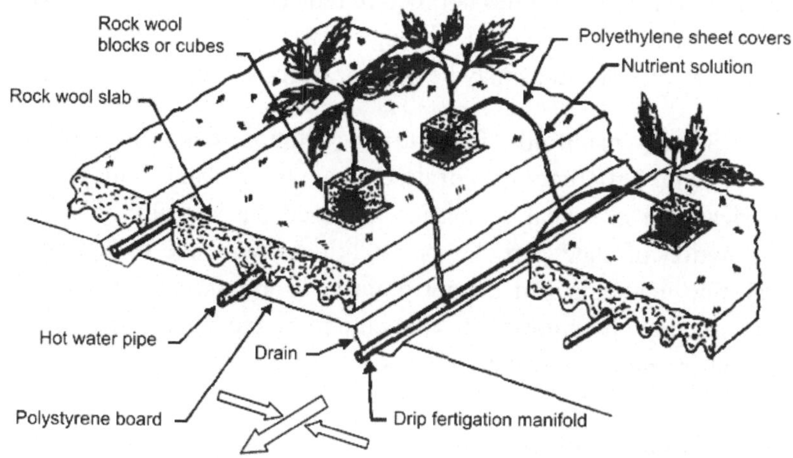

Fig. 19.4 A typical layout of open system of rock wool culture.

It can be incorporated as a soil amendment after crops are grown in greenhouse for several years. In addition, an open system with rock wool permits accurate and uniform delivery of nutrient solution, requires less equipment, fabrication, and installation costs, and entails less risk of crop failure due to the breakdown of pumps and recycling equipment. The obvious disadvantage is that the rock wool may be relatively costly unless manufactured within the region, and has disposal problem also as it is nondegradable.

19.1.4 Sand Culture

Concurrent with the beginning of rock wool culture in Denmark, a type of open-system aggregate hydroponics, initially for desert applications and using pure sand as the growing medium, was under development. As other types of growing media must be imported to desert regions and may require frequent renewal, they are more expensive than sand, a commodity usually available in abundance. When the growth of tomatoes and other greenhouse crops in pure sand was compared with the growth in nine other mixtures, there were no significant differences in yield. Unlike many other growing media, which undergo physical breakdown during use, sand is a permanent medium. It does not require replacement every one or two years. Pure sand can be used in trough or trench culture. The areas to be used as planting beds may be level or slightly sloped.

Supply manifolds for nutrient solution must be installed accordingly. Different types of desert and coastal sands with various physical and chemical properties are used successfully. The size distribution of sand particles is not critical, with the exception of very fine materials that do not drain well and should be avoided. The principal crops grown in sand culture systems are tomatoes and cucumbers, and yields of both crops are high.

19.2 Closed Systems

In closed systems of aggregate hydroponics, the recovered excess nutrient solution was recirculated in combination with the fresh solution after correction. When compared to the open system, closed systems activities are high intense, high technology oriented and require high cost investment. Elaborate arrangements of NFT will always be a part of closed aggregate hydroponic systems. In closed systems, special substrates, such as well graded gravel, which was popular in the past, and the rock wool are employed.

19.2.1 Gravel

Closed systems using gravel as the aggregate material were commonly employed for commercial and semi-commercial or family hydroponic CEA facilities 20 years ago. As in all closed systems, water analysis for agricultural suitability must be done. Great care must be taken to avoid the buildup of toxic salts and to keep the system free of nematodes and soil borne diseases. Once certain diseases are introduced, the infested nutrient solution will contaminate the entire planting. Such systems are capital intensive as they require leak proof growing beds, as well as subgrade mechanical systems and nutrient storage tanks. Gravel is not now recommended for use as an aggregate in a closed system, since the newer NFT systems have more advantages than gravel based installations.

19.2.2 NFT and Rock Wool

A more recent development in Europe is the combination of NFT and rock wool culture, which is a closed aggregate system. In this application, plants are established on small rock wool slabs positioned in channels containing recycled nutrient solution. Compared to the open rock wool system, this procedure reduces the amount of rock wool required, a definite advantage while disposing the used rock wool. The rock wool, in combination with the NFT systems, acts as a nutrient reservoir in case of pump failure and helps to anchor the plants in the nutrient channel. Since the cation$^+$ exchange capacity is negligible, applied nutrients are not adsorbed. Nutrient availability to plants is dictated only by the nutrient solution applied.

Horticultural rock wool is available in 18 to 100 mm cubes with or without predrilled holes for propagation of seeds or cuttings. The smaller cubes can be obtained unwrapped in blocks suitable for use in trays. Larger cubes are often wrapped on the vertical sides with polyethylene to prevent evaporation and spread of roots into adjacent cubes and are sold in single-row strips. Rock wool offers the following advantages:

1. In the case of NFT, pasteurization can be eliminated in rock wool culture.
2. Rock wool is an excellent inert substrate for open-system nutriculture.
3. Rock wool increases the production efficiency.
4. It is also possible to recirculate nutrient solution in a rock wool system.
5. Rock wool culture reduces the production space.
6. Rock wool is light in weight and self-contained.
7. Rock wool allows movement of plants into different environments and densities in different stages for faster crop production.

8. Rock wool system has low overhead cost.
9. Rock wool permits growth of crops on movable benches.

19.3 Whole-firm Recirculation

When a particular component in the effluent water is not allowed to be disposed in the usual manner by certain regulatory measures, one way of achieving this is to recirculate all the runoff water from firm known as whole-firm circulation. Plants in the greenhouse or the field are grown on a plastic-lined or paved surface. Plants can be grown in conventional containers and root substrates. Water or nutrient solution is applied in the conventional manner to the top of pot, flat, or bench if it is a fresh-flower crop.

Effluent passing out of the bottom of the container is caught on greenhouse floor and flows to a lined ditch. A network of ditches from each growing area carries the effluent collected from the entire to a set of settling ponds. Much of the sediment in the effluent settles out in those ponds. From these ponds, water is pumped to an equalization pond to establish an average level of fertilizer in the effluent coming from the previous applications of water or fertilizer to the crops. The effluent is tested for pH level and individual nutrient concentration. Alum is added as flocculent to settle the suspended solids. Chlorine treatment is given to pasteurize the clear effluent off the disease pathogens and to precipitate iron and manganese. Acid or base is added to adjust the pH level, and individual nutrient concentrates at appropriate proportions are added based on the tests before recirculation. This technique is in line with the recommendations of the pollution regulation laws, since the effluent the whole firm is recirculated and reduces the possible pollution of land or existing disposal stream.

REVIEW QUESTIONS

1. What are aggregate hydroponic systems? Bring out the similarities and differences between liquid hydroponic systems.

2. What are open hydroponic systems? Explain the nutrient introduction methods in open hydroponic systems with suitable diagrams.
3. Describe trough and trench culture with neat sketches.
4. Write a note on bag culture.
5. What is rock wool? How it is manufactured and what are the advantages?
6. With a layout diagram explain the rock wool culture.
7. Describe the method of sand culture.
8. Write about gravel type closed system of hydroponics.
9. Give an account on the NFT and rock wool culture in closed system of hydroponics.
10. Discuss about whole-firm recirculation.

Chapter 20

ECONOMICS OF GREENHOUSE PRODUCTION

Regardless of the type, protected agricultural systems are extremely expensive. The equipment and production cost may be more than compensated by the significantly higher productivity of protected agricultural systems as compared with OFA. The costs and returns of protected agriculture vary greatly, depending on the system used, the location and the crop grown. A 1993 estimate of such a total turnkey cost in Arizona, U. S. for a modern and sophisticated CEA system, exclusive of land and the interior growing system is $\$85/m^2$. By design, all protected agriculture systems of cropping are intensive in use of land, labour, and capital. Greenhouse agriculture is the most intensive system of all. The intensity of land use is greatly dependent upon the system of protected agriculture. Year-round greenhouse crop production is therefore much more intensive than seasonal use of mulches and row covers. Coinciding with intensity are yields, which are normally far greater per hectare from year-round than from seasonal systems. The normal benefits of higher yields of CEA over the OFA depend on the system used and the region of production. The various aspects of greenhouse production economics, such as capital requirements, production economics and the conditions influencing returns are described in the chapter.

20.1 Capital Requirements

The capital requirements differ greatly among the various systems of protected agriculture. Mulching is least expensive while greenhouses require the most capital per unit of land. Total cost involved in the production is the sum of fixed costs and operating costs (Fig. 20.1). The fixed capital costs include land, fixed and mobile equipment, and structures like grading, packing, and office. Fixed costs also include taxes and maintenance. The fixed capital costs for greenhouses clearly exceed those of other systems of protected agriculture, but vary in expense according to type of structure, and environmental control and growing systems. Operating or variable costs include labour, fuel, utilities, farm chemicals and packaging materials. The operating costs and fixed costs are annual expenditures and these can be substantial. Annual costs may correlate to some extent with capital investment. A more intensive culture is possible in a more advanced or intensive system of protected agriculture and the costs accrue proportionally. Since systems of protected agriculture differ greatly, each system, and its capital requirements, should be studied individually.

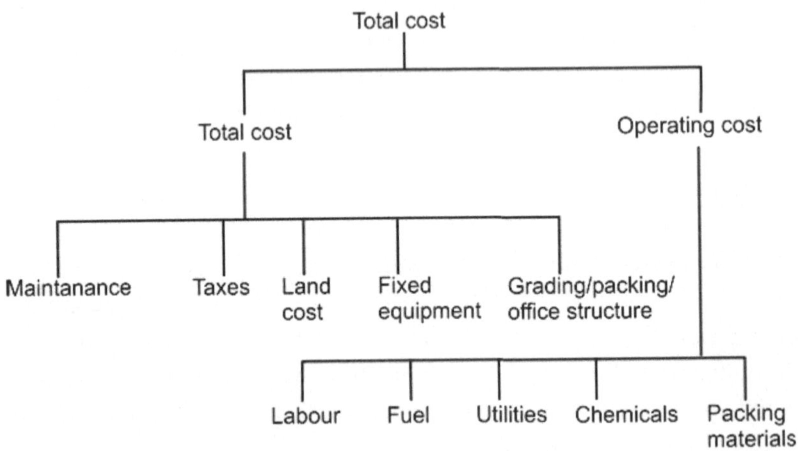

Fig. 20.1 Flow diagram of capital requirements of production.

Plastic mulchs and row covers normally cost* Rs. 1.7 to 2.6/m^2 depending on the row spacing, type of mulch, and the supplier. In estimating the capital requirements, the grower must include the cost of the entire system as well as the mulch. While greenhouse production systems may be far more expensive than open field systems of equal land area, open field systems of protected agriculture are normally more extensive in field area than in greenhouse production.

The high-tunnel growing unit, a simple structure with little environmental control equipment, is less expensive to build. Selecting such a unit reduces the amount of capital needed and the amortisation costs. For a high-tunnel polyethylene structures the cost of construction is approximately* Rs. 608/m^2 including cover, black plastic mulch on the floor and trickle irrigation. Greenhouses are expensive, especially if the environment is controlled by the use of heaters, fan and pad cooling systems, and computer controls. The cost of environment controlled greenhouse is approximately* Rs. 3392/m^2 (*Costs were based on 1985 USA price information and were furnished to provide a scenario).

20.2 Economics of Production

Production economics considers the various components of fixed and variable costs, compares them with the income and evaluates the net return, on unit area basis. On an average basis, wages account for approximately 85% of the total variable cost. Wages are the greatest expenditure in greenhouse production, followed by amortization costs and then energy costs. Energy expenditure will appear when heating is necessary. About two-fifths of the expenses are fixed costs and about three-fifths are variable costs. Depreciation and interest on investment account for most of the fixed costs.

20.3 Conditions Influencing Returns

A number of variables which may not show up in the yearly financial balance sheet influence the returns to greenhouse operators, such as economics of scale, physical facilities, cropping patterns and government incentives. The size of any system of protected agriculture will depend on the market objectives of the grower.

Most protected agricultural endeavours are family operated. Often the products are retailed directly to the consumer through a roadside market at the farm site. In the developed world, greenhouse operations tend to be of a size that can be operated by one family (0.4 to 0.8 ha). A unit of 0.4 ha can be operated by two to three labourers, with additional help at periods of peak activity. This amount of labour can usually be provided by the owner and his family. Moreover, the owner will pay close attention to management, which is the most important factor. Labour costs may rise significantly if it is necessary to recruit labour from outside the family. Greenhouse owners who hire a highly qualified manager may have to operate a larger than family-size greenhouse in order to offset the additional salary paid. The greenhouse system economy can be improved with increased size when:

1. There is a unique opportunity to mechanise certain operations.
2. Labour can be more efficiently utilized.
3. Low cost capital is available.
4. There are economics in the purchase of packaging materials and in marketing.
5. Some special management skills are available.

The physical facilities and location of the greenhouse influence economics. Another variable that influences the profits from the gree nhouses is intensity of production, which is determined by the type of structure. Using plastic mulches, high-tunnels, and the structures with complete environmental control system facilitate year-round production and early harvest, thus enabling the grower to realize higher profits. Year-round production offers year-round employment to the labourers.

It is found that the environmentally controlled greenhouse produced only one-third more revenue than the high-tunnel structure. With the improved transportation facilities, the new areas of production in combination with the following factors contribute to lower the costs:

1. High sunlight intensity undiminished by air pollution.
2. Mild winter temperatures.
3. Infrequent violent weather conditions.
4. Low humidity during the summer for cooling.
5. Availability of water with low salinity levels.

Cropping pattern will have bearing on the greenhouse structure. A high-tunnel structure or any structure not fitted with environmental control equipment for heating and cooling will be used only on a seasonal basis. It is common to switch over from greenhouse vegetable production to flower production, especially in structures with more elaborate environmental control systems. Growers throughout the world are currently experimenting with alternative crops, such as herbs. As eating habits change, with times and as the consumers are becoming increasingly conscious of diet and the nutritional value of fruits and vegetables, growers must continually look for alternatives to existing cropping patterns. Government policies also influence the financial returns from the crops. Governments may provide grants or low interest loans, subsidies towards construction costs, fuel, and use of plastics, such as drip irrigation systems, mulches, row covers, and covering materials. Such incentives from the government encourage the growers and stimulate the greenhouse industry.

REVIEW QUESTIONS

1. What are the components of capital requirements of greenhouse facility?
2. What are the constituents of economics of production?
3. Briefly discuss the conditions influencing the returns from greenhouse cultivation.

BIBLIOGRAPHY

Aldrich, R. A., and J. W. Bartok, Jr. 1994. *Greenhouse Engineering* (3rd Rev.). NRAES-33, Cornell University, Ithaca, New York, USA.

ASAE Standards. 2002. Sec. EP460. Commercial greenhouse design and layout. ASAE, St. Joseph, Michigan, USA.

Bohanon, H. R., C. E. Rahilly, and J. Stout. 1993. *The Greenhouse Climate Control Handbook*. Acme Eng. And Manufacturing Corp, Form C7S, Muskogee, Oklahoma, USA.

Boodley, J. W. 1996. *The Commercial Greenhouse* (2nd Ed.). Delmar Publishers, Albany, New York, USA.

Briassoulis, D., D. Waaijenberg, J. Gratraud, and B. Von Eslner. 1997. Mechanical properties of covering materials for greenhouses: Part 1, General Overview. *Journal of Agricultural Engineering Research* 67: 81-96.

CAST. 1975. Potential for Energy Conservation in Agricultural Production. CAST Report 40, Ames, Iowa, USA.

Electricity Council. 1972. *Growelectric Handbook No. 2: Lighting in Greenhouse*. Electricity Council, Millbank, London, UK.

http://mathforum.org/dr.math/faq/faq.circle.segment.html#8 of http://mathforum.org/drexel/. Accessed on May, 2006.

Jasen, M. H., and A. J. Malter. 1985. Hydroponic Vegetable Production. *Horticultural Review* 7: 1-44, 483-558.

Kholliev, B. Ch., T. Jadikov, and B. V. Khairitdinov. 1982. On the investigation of solar hot house/fruit dryer. *Applied Solar Energy* 18(3): 67-69.

Langhans, R.W. 1990. *Greenhouse Management – A guide to structures, environmental control, materials handling, crop programming and business analysis* (3rd Ed.). Halcyon Press of Ithaca, New York, USA.

National Greenhouse Manufacturers Association. 2004. *Standards: Design loads in greenhouse structures, ventilating and cooling greenhouses, greenhouse heat loss, statement of policy – greenhouse retrofit.* NGMA, Littleton, Colorado, USA.

Nelson, P. V. 2003. *Greenhouse Operation & Management.* 6th Ed. Prentice Hall, Upper Saddle River, New Jersey, USA.

Papadikas, G., A. Frangoudakis, and S. Kyritis. 1981. Soil energy balance analysis of a solar greenhouse. *Journal of Agricultural Engineering Research* 43: 231-243.

Pitam Chandra, J. K. Singh, and G. Majumdar. 1989. Some results of evaporative cooling a plastic greenhouse. *ISAE Journal of Agricultural Engineering* 26: 274-281.

Radha Manohar, K. 1993. An experimental study on drying of agricultural produce in greenhouse type solar dryer using stack effect for ventilation. Unpublished M.Sc. Thesis, Indian Agricultural Research Institute, New Delhi, India.

Souvenier on National on Commercialization of Tissue Culture and Greenhouse Technology. 1995. Bangalore (5-6 May). National Committee on the Use of Plastics in Agriculture, Ministry of Agriculture, Government of India, New Delhi, India.

Tiwari, K. N. 1995. *Manual of Drip Irrigation, Greenhouse and Plastic Mulching.* Plasticulture Development Centre, Department of Agriculture and Food Engineering, IIT, Kharagpur, India.

Wells, O. S., and J. B. Loy. 1985. Intensive vegetable production with row covers. *HortiScience* 20: 822-826.

Willits, D. H. 1993. *Greenhouse Cooling.* North Carolina Flower Growers Bulletin 38: 15-18.

Wooden Structured Greenhouse. 1991. Do-It-Yourself Manual. Plasticulture, Indian Petrochemicals Corporation Limited, India.

INDEX

A

Acrylic rigid panel 60
Active cooling 12
Active heating 12
Active summer cooling 86
Active winter cooling 94
Advantages of greenhouse 5
Aeroponics 189
A-frame greenhouse 9
A-frame, aeroponics 190
Aggregate hydroponics 193
Air removal ratings 91
Air infiltration 100
Air removal, adjusted 89
Air removal, standard 88
Air supported row covers 167
Amortization cost 207
Application efficiency 140
Arch roof 45
Area of pad 91

B

Bag culture, hydroponics 196
Biodegradable mulches 155
Biological controls 132
Bitumen 79
Black LDPE film 79
Boom watering 139
Burial of mulches 158

C

California system 162
Capital requirements 206
Carbon dioxide generator 30
Carbon dioxide levels 21
Carbon dioxide sensor 31
Carbon dioxide tester 31
CAST 106
Cast concrete modified NFT 180
Central heating system 101
Central Tobacco Research Institute 145
Cheese cloth 129
Chimney effect 35
Chlorine treatment 202
Chord 13
Classification of greenhouses 7
Closed hydroponic system 200
Computer control advantages 41
Computers 39
Conditions influencing returns 207
Conduction loss 100
Controlled environmental agriculture 3, 177, 205
Convection loss 100
Convection tube 94, 103
Cooling pads 37
Creosote 79
Cross connectors 72
Cross-fluted cellulose pads 25, 90

Cultural procedures, NFT 183
Curing of tobacco 144

D

Dead air space 100
Deep flow hydroponics 186
Definition of greenhouse 1
Design loads 45
DIF 126
Disposal of mulches 157
Dissolved oxygen 180
Drip emitters 140
Drip irrigation 140
Dynamic root floating hydroponics 187

E

Economics of production 207
Effect of carbon dioxide 21
Effect of light 18
Effect of relative humidity 20
Effect of temperature 20
Effect of ventilation 21
Effluent 202
Electro-galvanizing 51
Elevation factor 86
Enzymes 20
Equalization pond 202
Evaporative cooling 25
Even span type greenhouse 8
Excelsior pads 25, 91
Exhaust fan 89

F

Fan and pan cooling 25, 37
Fan spacing 89
Fernhurst system 164
Fertilizer proportioners 194
Fixed cost 206
Flat plate solar collector 104
Floating row covers 170
Flocculent 202
Floricultural crop requirements 130
Fog cooling system 26
Fogging system 26, 37
Foliage diseases 131
Foundation pipes 69
Frost protection 166
FRP rigid pane 59
Functions of mulches 150
Fungal diseases 131

G

Galvanized iron 51
Genetic control 133
GI wire network 81
Glass greenhouse construction 65
Gothic arch 45
Gravel culture, hydroponics 200
Greenhouse effect 4
Greenhouse type solar dryer 144

H

Hammered glass 52
Hand watering 136
Heat conservation practice 106
Heat distribution systems 103
Heat loss modes 100
Heating systems 101
Herbicide films 155
HID lamps 129
History of greenhouse 1
Hoops 68
Horizontal air flow, HAF 28
Horticultural grade rock wool 198, 201
Hot dip galvanizing 51
Hydroponic system 175
Hydroponics, CEA 177

I

Incineration of mulches 158
Inclined panel 190
Infrared transmitting mulches 154
Infrared absorbing polyethylene 57
Insect traps 133
Integrated pest management, IPM 132

L

Lateral supports 69
Lean-to type greenhouse 8
Light factor 87
Light intensity 18
Light intensity requirements 127, 130
Light quality 128
Lighting systems 129
Lux 18

M

Manual controlling 24
Microprocessor 38
Moisture stress 136
Movable channels NFT 181
Moving belt NFT 182
Mulch laying techniques 157

N

Natural mulches 152
Natural ventilation 34
NFT advantages 182, 200
NGMA 86
Nutriculture 175
Nutrient film technique, NFT 178
Nutrient mixing tank 194
Nutrient pool 186
Nutrient solution 178
Nutrient solution concentration 183

O

Open field agriculture, OFA 177
Open hydroponic systems 194
Operating cost 206
Orientation of greenhouse 44
Overhead sprinklers 138

P

Pad water delivery 91
Paper mulches 152
Paper tent cover 162
Perforated plastic tunnel 165
Perimeter watering 137
Pest and disease control methods 132
Pest and diseases 131
Petroleum mulches 152
Photodegradable films 155
Photoperiodism 128
Photosynthesis 17
Photosynthetically active radiation 57
Pipe boom 138
Pipe framed greenhouse construction 67
Pipe framed structures 13
Pipe system NFT 181
Plastic covered trench system 169
Plastic mulches 154
Plastic mulches advantages 155
Plug trays 139
Polycarbonate panel 60
Polyester film 58
Polyethylene film 56
Polyethylene mulches 153
Polygrip mechanism 69
Polypropylene sutli 79
Polypropylene twine 164
Polystyrene floats 186
Polyvinyl chloride, PVC film 57
Pressurizing fan 27
Pump capacity 93
PVC panel 59

Q

Quonset type greenhouse 10

R

Radiation heating system 102
Radiation loss 100
Requirements of mulches 151
Research needs 146
Ridge and furrow type greenhouse 9
Ridge line mechanism 69
Rock storage 104
Rock wool advantages 201
Rock wool culture hydroponics 197
Rock wool production 197
Roll-up door flap 83
Row cover polymer requirements 173
Rules of watering 135

S

Sand culture, hydroponics 199
Sash bar 66
Saw tooth type greenhouse 10
Scaffoldings 145
Sensible heat 20
Service buildings 64
Shading compounds 128
Shading methods 128
Shapes of greenhouse 7
Single drawn glass 52
Site selection 44
Slitted row cover 166
Soil ridges 169
Solar air collector 104
Solar heating system 103
Source of nutrients 185
Spectrum of light 19
Spray nozzle 26, 137
Spunbonded fabrics 170
Standards of glass fixing 52
Strut 13
Sump volume 92, 94
Sun drying 143
Sun screen 129
Supplemental lighting 129
Surfactants 198

T

Tefzel T^2 film 58
Temperature factor 87
Tempered glass 52
Thermal blanket 129
Thermister 24
Thermo plastics 56
Thermocouple 24
Thermopane glasses 12
Thermostat 24
Tobacco curing stages 145
Trough and trench culture hydroponics 195
Truss framed structures 13

U

Ultraviolet stabilized LDPE 67
Ultraviolet stabilized polyethylene 57
Uneven span type greenhouse 9
Unit heater 101

V

Velocity factor 88

W

Wages 207
Water storage 104
Whole firm circulation 202
Winter factor 94
Wire hoop 162
Wood 49
Wood preservatives 50
Wooden framed structures 12
Wooden stakes 162
Wooden support blocks 8